THE JOY OF NEGATIVE THINKING

Donald G. Smith

Delancey Press

PHILADELPHIA, PA

11463

Grateful acknowledgment is made for the opening quote to Chapter 6, which is reprinted with permission from the November 1991 *Reader's Digest* and the July 1991 issue of *The Freeman.*

Published by:
Delancey Press
P.O. Box 40285
Philadelphia, PA 19106

Library of Congress Catalog Card Number: 94-70571
ISBN: 0-9627935-6-6

Manufactured in the United States of America.
5 4 3 2 1

Printed on acid-free paper.
Printed and bound by Versa Press, Inc.

Cover and book design by Robert LeBrun.

Also by Donald G. Smith:
How To Cure Yourself Of Positive Thinking
And They Also Kick You When You're Down

To all the world's leaned-upon.
To the leaners, a plague upon your houses.

Contents

Introduction

Let's start with a premise: the world is essentially a good place, and life is good. If this book has a message, this is it.

Assuming this to be true, we must then ask ourselves why there is so much unhappiness in the world, so much misery and injustice. This is an easy one, however. It is because we *allow* it to happen. We let the serpents into the garden when they have no business being there.

Happiness is not a tangible thing that we seek as though it were the Holy Grail. Happiness is nothing more than the absence of unhappiness, which means that if we can get rid of all the disruptive elements in our lives—things, situations, people—we can achieve the norm, which is happiness. The big advantage is that we are working with a sliding scale, so we don't have to face an all-or-nothing proposition. If we drive only half of the snakes from the garden, then we are 50% better off than we were, and 90% is sheer bliss, far better than any of us can reasonably expect.

Given the choice, it is better to give up something that we want than to have something thrust on us that we don't. For example, if I won a free trip to the Bahamas, I would give it up in a second if by so doing I could avoid a 3-day orgy of watching someone else's vacation slides. I would gladly give up an evening with good friends if it meant a corresponding session with ignorant louts. I would give up lobster to avoid eating Spam, a week in Beverly Hills to crawl out of a week in Newark, an hour of hearing the angels playing their golden harps to avoid a lecture on insurance or dental hygiene.

This is truly the secret of happiness, and all human happiness is somehow interlaced with that wonderful word *No*. No, you cannot live with us. No, I will not give you a thin dime. No, you cannot borrow my car, and no, you will not sing at my wedding.

Admittedly, the word *No* is a hard thing to say, especially the first time. The rewards are so great, however, that it is well worth the trouble. By learning to say this simple word and then standing by your decision, we can lead lives of guaranteed contentment and enjoy every glorious day to the fullest. Life is not a matter of getting or acquiring, but rather of avoiding and preventing. We start living when we learn to say *No*.

POSITIVE THINKING: IT STILL DOESN'T WORK

How did positive thinking come to be synonymous with the Holy Word? How can it perpetuate itself when it has such a sorry track record; promising so much and delivering so little?

HOW TO CURE YOURSELF OF POSITIVE THINKING

In 1976, I published a book called *How To Cure Yourself Of Positive Thinking.* It was prompted by my strong dislike for the positive-thinking twaddle that had been making the rounds for a considerable time even then and, unfortunately, was influencing people who should have known better.

The book sold reasonably well, and I did a bit of publicity touring for it. I also received a lot of hate mail from people who somehow equated positive thinking with Christianity and who accused me of being some sort of anti-Christian devil worshiper. They defended their own piety by calling me obscene names in their unsigned letters.

My chief objections to the overly simplistic—and rather idiotic—positive-thinking philosophy were and still are:

  1. Too often it is used as a manipulative tool to keep subordinates in line.

2. It is an unworkable, completely ineffectual bit of chicanery that always fails the poor, sad people who need help the most.

The manipulative aspect of positive thinking is obvious. The superior–subordinate relationship can be reinforced quite respectably by a call for "a good, positive attitude," which sounds much better than ordering an intelligent person to support a bad idea. In business, the person who objects to a godawful plan of action is labeled *negative*, which is a lot better than saying he opposes something that is patently dumb.

Positive thinking simply does not work, primarily because it is based on an absurdity that precludes any possibility of success. In most cases, this isn't especially dangerous. Unfortunately, it is offered to people who are looking for help and is about as effective as a rain dance during a drought. Thinking *good* thoughts will not make something happen, and it is only a little short of cruel to tell someone anything different.

The positive-thinking philosophy also assumes we have a control over our lives that really does not exist. Much of what happens to us is decided by people whom we don't know, sitting in conference rooms in distant cities. Take job security, for example. Almost every working man and woman has either experienced a layoff or at least worried about involuntary unemployment from the great axe of the "personnel cutback." This is a cold, highly impersonal thing and is brought about by forces unknown to the affected workers and dictated by people whom they do not know and will never meet. It is simply decided by someone, somewhere, that a given percentage of all employees will be unemployed on a certain date, but *you* have lost your job. Positive thinking isn't going to prevent it, and neither will incantations, candles, incense, nor animal sacrifice.

Mortgage rates are beyond our control as well. So are loan decisions, petroleum prices, medical test results, insurance policy cancellations, and winning lottery numbers. Some of the most important things affecting our lives are completely beyond our influence, yet the positive-thinking fraternity chooses to ignore this and tell us that a "good attitude" is going to make a big difference in the way these things are decided.

Even with the things we do control, performance counts for much more than attitude. A good example is my California adult teaching credential. I had been teaching management courses for several years in private industry when I discovered that I could teach in the public school system if I acquired a state credential. To do this, I had to undergo two 3-unit courses, which took place in all-day, Saturday sessions lasting for a total of 12 weeks—a dozen straight Saturdays in the life of a working person who valued a free Saturday about as much as anyone can value anything.

I wasn't even halfway through the first session when I realized that the whole thing was going to be a waste of time and was valuable only as a means to an end. We were required to sit in a large circle and to "share" our experiences, something of a grown-up show-and-tell. Sometimes we acted out little playlets dealing with the teaching situation. In that my classmates would be teaching such diverse courses as auto-brake repair, dog grooming, oriental cooking, wood carving, and in my case, English and writing, the playlets had no applicability whatsoever and served little purpose other than to fill a long, long Saturday session.

So, here we come to the subject of attitude, which is the very soul of positive thinking. I could have attended these interminable sessions with a smile and full of enthusiasm, or endured them as I did, as an ordeal I had to suffer through to get my credential. For those who would interject that I might have done better in the courses with an improved attitude, I can report that I received an *A* in both, primarily because I knew what kind of drivel they expected and gave it to them. (I used the word *share* a lot.)

I cite this example only to show that *attitude* has little to do with *accomplishment*. A mature person knows what must be done to get where he wants to be—in this case, surrendering 12 precious days-off to be able to teach in the public school system. I am no better a teacher for the experience, and I gained absolutely nothing from the courses. It had to be done, however, and I did it, not cheerfully but neither with any whimpering nor foot-dragging. And so it is in life.

There is also the mistaken belief that *positive* resides on a higher ethical level than *negative*. Thus, we speak of a "good, positive attitude" as though *good* and *positive* naturally belong together, but where is the evidence to support this conclusion? A positive thinker might easily be a sniveling sycophant, a poorly educated and woefully misinformed person, an egomaniacal public-relations type with something to sell, or merely a good-natured imbecile.

Positive thinking is certainly the stuff of small minds, and it is tailored to reach people who do not run the risk of overtaxing their thought processes. It represents an *in-lieu-of* philosophy, which in this case replaces the necessity for either logical thought or formal education, and it appeals to those who come up short in both areas and are too lazy to do anything about either one. Why read Plato, Aquinas, Locke, Hegel, Kant, and Dewey when all one really needs to do is rub the magic lamp and apply this simplistic bit of jingoism to get a firm hold on life? Why study, why read, why expand one's knowledge? With positive thinking, one doesn't have to dig, to compare, to analyze, or to question—only to accept something that was created for a 10-year-old intellect as an eternal truth, then put all mental energies at eternal rest.

Nor is negative thinking entirely a bad thing. In fact, in an atmosphere where bad ideas abound, such as the applied sycophancy of private industry and the self-entrenching battlefront of the public sector, negativism should be a vital factor in keeping the ship afloat. Often, the greatest thing you can accomplish in a given day is to kill a bad idea, with the second greatest being to wound it severely and send it off into the bush.

It has been the better part of two decades since I launched my first attack on positive thinking, and I confess that I have seen little in the way of tangible results. Perhaps it would have been different if my target had been an identifiable, fire-breathing dragon, but I have been devoting my time to attacking the ramparts of applied silliness, which is a slippery foe indeed.

Positive thinking is not the business of the scholar, the semi-scholar, or the awakening intellect. Rather, it is the direct sale of pap from one small mind to another. It is not bad, just ridiculous, and if I can sell this one, simple message, I will have slain my own dragon.

PROBLEM PERENNIALS

True friendship is never based on need. A real friend is someone who doesn't want—or expect—anything from you.

Those who talk about sharing problems have little grounding in the realities of existence. Ideally, I tell you my problems today, you tell me your problems tomorrow, we help each other, and we are both the better for it. Unfortunately, it doesn't work this way.

The truth is that precious little problem "sharing" goes on in the world. Rather, there are the *dumpers* and the *dumpees*. People who consistently listen to other people's problems rarely have the opportunity to unload on anyone else. Conversely, the *Problem Perennials* are forever unloading on anyone who will listen (or who lacks the dexterity to slip out of the corner).

A Problem Perennial is someone who *always* has a problem and *always* wants to involve someone else. Often, he is a moocher. He needs a ride, a "small" loan, a place to stay, or maybe to borrow your camera, your typewriter, or your vacuum cleaner. Whatever it might be, the moocher *wants* something.

In other cases, the Problem Perennial is the personification of a mismanaged life. This loser is always one short step ahead of the bill collectors and the lawyers, drives with a suspended license, owes everyone in town, and can't keep a job. The current problem is the result of the perpetual "mistake." The bank mixed up the account. The police report was in error. The boss blamed the wrong person. The witness was lying. This loser is forever the victim of the "mistake." Oddly enough, however, these mistakes never seem to plague the rest of us.

No matter how the problems manifest themselves, there are several distinguishable characteristics that bind all Problem Perennials into one big, undesirable lump:

1. *They never learn.* This one is truly constant. There are people still unborn who will be buying lightning-rod franchises. The subcretin who makes stupid investments and loses his shirt at 25 will be surrendering the same shirt at 70, still trying for that big score. The woman married to a husband who comes home drunk and beats her will eventually divorce him, then marry a man who—guess what?—comes home drunk and beats her. The hypochondriac who receives neither attention nor sympathy from fancied illnesses will continue indefinitely with the routine, each time gaining nothing from it. Problem Perennials almost always are repeaters, and they learn absolutely nothing from experiences that should be sufficient even for preschoolers.

2. *They are constantly in need.* Probably the most annoying trait of the Problem Perennial is that

he always wants something. No matter what course the conversation takes, there is always the bubbling pot just below the surface. The person who is going to hit you up for money, or anything else, will go along with sports, politics, or what-good-books-have-you-read for just so long, then comes to the bite. This is the primary reason that nobody wants these people around: they can't walk away without something from you.

3. *They are oblivious to other people's needs.* A Problem Perennial doesn't care one iota if you can afford to give him the money, or if it is going to be an inconvenience to drive him someplace. He doesn't care if you have to miss a day of work to tend to his needs, or if you don't want him driving your car. The telephone marathoner doesn't care in the least that his victim might have something else to do. The loser with one long marital problem has no interest in learning that somebody doesn't want to listen to it. Other people's interests and needs are of no concern at all.

4. *They have to bring other people into their misery.* Problem Perennials are vitally concerned with one-way sharing. Whatever the problem, anyone within a 5-mile radius must be a part of it. Here we see the drunk who cannot drink alone, or the neglected spouse who wants to harangue the world with an endless monologue. Nor can we overlook that bundle of cheer still telling her grown children about the agonies of child-birth and how she suffered bringing them into the world. These people also wonder why they aren't invited anywhere.

5. *They cannot see the obvious.* People who habitually talk a problem into the ground can never see

that they aren't the most popular people to have around. They often complain that they spend too much time alone and that no one *cares*. They don't realize that they are extremely depressing people and that others might want to laugh once in awhile (or at least come up for air). It is a simple fact of life that most people do not want to spend an eternity dealing with someone else's problems.

6. *They can tune any subject into the "problem channel."* The person who has come to air his problems is going to do it, no matter what. A discussion on grain subsidies, for example, might bring out the following response: "George and I were discussing that very subject the day before he ran off with that tramp and left me with three children to raise." Or, "That no good lying boss of mine used to write letters to the paper about grain subsidies. He fired me because he knew that I had the goods on him." (Or the ever popular, "I have a good book on that subject, but I've been too sick to read it.") These people can do the same with nuclear disarmament, euthanasia, animal experimentation, and the relative advantages and disadvantages of term life insurance. A real professional can even sense a drift in topics and flawlessly steer the conversation right back to the fleeing husband and the vengeful employer.

7. *They are unscrupulous.* Every Problem Perennial comes equipped with a "lever," which they use to exploit blood relationships, old friendships, school ties, even presumably God and the flag. These people will use every known ploy to make you act in their interests. The answer is to remain firm. Any sign of weakening will bring

on a full attack, and the slightest rift often leads to total collapse. These people are cagey foes indeed, and they know how to make it past the moat and into your castle.

8. *They don't want their problems solved.* These people have learned to treasure their problems like collections of fine Dresden china or Hummel figurines. They love their problems, and above all, they *need* them. Problems are their only link with mankind. The Problem Perennial sees complaining as communication; to talk is to gripe. Problems are their world, so don't talk to them about solutions. They don't want to hear it.

Remember that we are not talking about people with normal—and therefore solvable—problems. We are discussing people with chronic problems, usually self-made, that will never go away. These people are determined to keep the pot boiling, and there is no defense against them except the word *No.*

An interesting thing about this word is the great sense of relief that it brings once it is spoken. The hours before this great oral delivery can be stressful and taxing. Many people have spent sleepless nights because the morning was going to bring about a confrontation with a Problem Perennial with an impossible request. Yet, once the word is spoken, once it is out in the air, one wonders why all of the stress was necessary. It is truly one of life's most rewarding moments when you muster the strength to say *No* to an undeserving wretch.

A lot of this stress can be attributed directly to the lever that the Problem Perennial is applying. Often, it is a family tie or some other personal bond that is supposed to work on the emotions and make you act in an illogical manner. There are also societal influences, and these have gone a *long* way to keep the professional moochers in fighting trim.

A case of the "old-town tie" occurred a few years ago with Nora. Nora received a phone call one morning from a woman named Daphne, whom Nora had known (but not all that well) during her high-school years in Minnesota. Daphne, a single woman in her forties, had just arrived in town—had in fact moved there—and wanted to "get together." Nora invited her over, they spent a few pleasant hours reminiscing about mutual friends, and Daphne stayed for dinner. She was also back the next night, and at least three nights a week from that point on. When Nora and her husband, Bill, went out to dinner, Daphne went along, and when they stayed home, Daphne was there, too. They had clearly become a threesome.

When Bill started to complain that he had had about enough of Daphne, the explanation was always, "Be patient. She's new in town and doesn't know anyone." After a year, however, it became readily apparent that Daphne had no interest in meeting anyone or in getting a life of her own. Her problem was and always would be that she didn't know anyone, but as long as she had Nora and Bill, she wouldn't even make the effort. She would never solve her problem, because she didn't want it solved. The "old friendship" was fictionalized to the point that she and Nora were inseparable as teenagers, when the truth was they had hardly knew each other then.

By this time, Nora had clearly reached the end of her tether but had no idea how to handle the situation. Bill stepped in and settled it for her. He told Daphne to back off and give them some space, and also to find a life of her own that didn't involve them. Daphne, incensed, quit her job and moved back to Minnesota, firmly believing that Bill had maliciously broken up an old friendship. Of course, this was not true, but there is one thing he did accomplish: he got Daphne off their backs forever.

We hear a lot about *understanding* these days. We are supposed to understand the problems of our fellow beings, then act in a way that no sane person could ever justify. When used in this way, the word is meant to imply *approval*, which isn't the case at all. So, let us dispense with that notion now and forever. Understanding has nothing to do with approval.

People during World War II certainly understood Adolf Hitler as much as they understood Winston Churchill and Pope Pius XII. There was no lack of understanding for Judas Iscariot, Jack the Ripper, Al Capone, or the Freeway Strangler. These people were understood completely. Now, understanding in no way implies approval, but the social do-gooders would have us believe that if we *understand* a person, then we will want to *act* in that person's behalf (i.e., give money to someone who is going to flush it down the sewer, or spend an evening listening to an account of a self-made problem). Thus, we are left with the scenario that we must listen to these people, and by so doing, we are obligated to help them. But, whoever listens to the listeners? (Most assuredly not the Problem Perennials.)

All of this leads to the matter of what we really owe the people who make demands on us. We should start by understanding the difference between a *responsibility* and an *obligation*. A responsibility is an accountability, usually moral, for behaving in a certain way. We are responsible for the welfare and happiness of our spouses, our children, and to a lesser extent, our elderly parents. We also have a responsibility to be good neighbors and good citizens. We are not responsible for our grown children, distant cousins, the guy across the street, and old Little League teammates.

An obligation is a somewhat different thing. Here we are talking about a binding promise, a good example being a formal debt. When we borrow money, we sign a paper agreeing to the terms of the loan and are obligated to repay it. Employment is also largely a matter of obligation. On accepting a job, we agree to work certain hours at a specified salary and to perform in a manner consistent with the standards of the workplace.

The mature person understands both responsibilities and obligations—and spends a lifetime meeting them. This person also understands those things that are neither responsibilities nor obligations and will not accept a debt that clearly is not his. Those who didn't cause the mess aren't responsible for the clean-up.

When the Problem Perennial stands on the doorstep with a heart-wrenching story and a hand already halfway into your wallet, ask yourself about responsibilities and obligations. Are you responsible for this person's welfare? Is there any reason that you are morally bound to keep this person afloat? If the answer is *No*, then have you signed any papers (or even agreed with a handshake) that you will be on hand to alleviate this person's problems? If the answer is still *No*, then you have scored a double "no-way" and are out of it completely. The next step is to get this point across.

One of the favorite ploys of the Problem Perennial is to back his mark into a corner and attempt to leave him no way out. For instance, "I have to come up with $714.18 by midnight, or my family will be put out onto the streets and I will be marched to the stockade and trampled to death by wild horses." Well, if the half-wit could see this coming, why didn't he look for advice a long time ago? This is a common procedure with the Problem Perennial. He never recognizes his own weakness and therefore doesn't look for advice to prevent the inevitable catastrophe. Instead, he mismanages right down the line, tells no one, then expects a bailout from someone else once he has run out of options.

If I could ever instill a single attitude into anyone, it would be a profound resentment at being backed into a corner and then (seemingly) given no choice but to respond as directed. For example, "If you do not take out a mortgage on your home and get me out of the country, I will have to go to prison for 10 years." For my part, I would refuse on the sole grounds of resentment, because anyone who would presume that I could be so misused and manipulated deserves no consideration whatever. If one wants to drop to a secondary consideration, however, there is the indisputable knowledge that this person is guilty of some transgression and indeed deserves to go to prison. *You* didn't commit the crime, so why are *you* paying for it?

Still another factor is the inevitable hardship that your family will suffer if you plunge deeper into debt. Why should your spouse and children suffer from the added financial burden while this loser escapes justice in Pago Pago or the Australian Outback? The answer clearly is that none of you should pay the price. Put your priorities in order, and let this disgusting individual eat prison food for awhile.

Morality is a cloudy thing indeed, and we often find ourselves groping for the *right* thing to do. Too often, we grope in the wrong direction and make a holy hash out of virtue. When we talk about helping our fellow man—or *caring*, as the popular notion is expressed— we often take this as a blanket moral dictum: we must help anyone and everyone who is in trouble, even if it means hurting those people who have done nothing wrong. This, of course, is absolute rubbish.

We are only obligated to help those people who deserve our help, and even then only when we can do so without hurting the people closest to us. The

Problem Perennials certainly do not fall into this category, and it is essential that we alone make this judgment. The person with his hand out does not make the determination of worthiness. Even if it is decided that the person is worthy, we must then determine if such help would bring about a hardship on innocent people, such as our immediate families. Saying *No*, however, often brings about feelings of guilt, because we have been conditioned to feel guilty about refusing anyone.

Let us remember—and never forget—that Problem Perennials thrive on other people's guilt. They cannot exist without it. They have to convince the rest of us that "less fortunate" includes those people who blew their rent money at the race track or snorted it up their noses, or maybe they bought things they couldn't afford and are now facing payback time. The person who refuses to work is not "less fortunate." Neither is the one who is fired regularly for excessive absenteeism. People who bring on their own misfortunes, usually after repeated warnings, are not to be pitied and are undeserving of anyone's compassion. There are too many deserving and legitimately needy people for anyone to be wasting time and money on those who repeatedly bring down the world on themselves.

This reminds me of another sad story, because it involved some very nice people. Chuck and Peggy lived in a cul-de-sac street in Los Angeles, filled with starter homes for young couples who hoped to move on to something better. Chuck was an aeronautical engineer, making a better-than-average salary and with prospects of living a long and comfortable life. Peggy worked as a technical writer and also earned a reasonably good salary. Like most young couples, they looked forward to children, a better house, and maybe seeing Paris before they died. The only flaw in this plan was Peggy's brother, Larry, a lifelong loser whose sole function in life seemed to be showing up at Chuck and Peggy's doorstep several times a year and mooching money, favors, and "a place to stay until I can get back on my feet."

Chuck eventually grew tired of this constant albatross around his neck and told Larry *No*, which Peggy resented. As she said, "He *is* my brother." She also kept on sending him money, but without telling Chuck. Eventually, and inevitably, however, Chuck found out. They argued, and they finally divorced, with brother Larry the sole cause.

Today, more than 25 years later, Chuck is remarried—his wife is an only child, incidentally—and Peggy lives alone in Los Angeles. She still gives regular handouts to Larry ("After all, he *is* my brother.") and looks forward to the day when Larry will get back on his feet and start catching a few of those good breaks that seem to come to everyone else.

Peggy is the personification of the professional mark. Larry has known all his life that there will always be "something in the well." With his younger sister, there will always be a financial handout, a meal, a place to stay, someone to lie for him and not condemn him for being the loathsome parasite he is. Peggy benefits by escaping guilt, and this is exactly the way Larry wants it. The more guilt that Peggy feels, the better it is for him. (The only big winner is Chuck, who is out of the whole sick thing forever.)

Another family story I've come across involves Andy, who also had a brush with a Problem Perennial. Andy is now an architect in Seattle, but his story starts in Los Angeles at a time when he had been divorced for about 5 years. When he met Marcy, a photographer and an attractive, extremely personable young woman, it seemed to be obvious from the beginning that they were a perfect match. In fact, they were engaged when they had known each other for only a few months.

There was a strange piece to the puzzle, however. Marcy was never able to be with Andy on Sundays, and after some intense questioning, Andy learned that she, her two brothers, and their wives were expected to be at "Daddy's" graveside. This Sunday gathering of the clan was a regular event. Mother demanded it, and no excuses were accepted. The woman could not let go. Therefore, no one else was allowed to either, and the entire family went as a sop to the mother's hang-up. When this woman expressed grief, she expected a cheering section. For Marcy, it was a 60-mile drive each way, but she hadn't missed a Sunday in the 7 years since her father had shuffled off this mortal coil.

When all of this business finally came out into the open, Marcy went a step further. She told Andy that he would be expected to participate after they were married. This rang an immediate bell in Andy's head: no Sunday golf, no weekend trips, and no goofing off around the apartment pool. Even more, he resented the fact that it was *expected*. Andy thought about it for all of 15 seconds and told Marcy that he was not about to spend his Sundays sitting in a cemetery. They argued, broke up, but eventually got back together when Marcy realized what it meant to be an adult. She told her mother that she would no longer be part of this Sunday sickness, and she has never regretted it. She and Andy have been married over 8 years now, and Mother (so far as I know) has survived this mutiny in her ranks.

We often make the mistake of believing that we can compromise our way to happiness. You give, I give, we meet somewhere in the middle, and everyone goes away happy. This sometimes works when we are buying a used car, but a society does not work this way. It is a sunshine philosophy, and such thinking always breaks down because it doesn't include people in the formula—in this case, people with a steamroller mentality. The Problem Perennials do not believe in compromise, because it puts them out of business. Their entire existence is based on their problems taking precedence over all things. When this is challenged, they lose. Theirs is a risky business, but to them, the fight is worth it. Losing means total, crushing defeat and (even worse) the possibility they might have to start living (and even thinking) like normal people. This won't do for them at all.

Problem Perennials have ruined more lives than all of the dictators, racketeers, terrorists, and serial killers combined. These people live by keeping everyone else in line, and there is no way to reason with them. They don't give an inch because they can't.

Trying to reach an accommodation with Problem Perennials has been about as successful as man's eternal battle against cockroaches and gophers. Man isn't winning. There are only two courses of action in dealing with these people. We can play it their way and spend a lifetime both supporting them and listening to an eternal monologue about how society has done them wrong. Or, we can say *No* and walk away.

Remember that a Problem Perennial is someone with no other interest in life beyond his own problems. He introduces the subject, won't get off the subject, and rejects all suggested solutions. Anyone who meets these simple conditions qualifies as a true Problem Perennial and must be dealt with accordingly. These people aren't going to change, so the strategy of waiting them out and hoping for the best really isn't an option. *You* have to change things, distasteful as that might sound, and this is accomplished only by employing that wonderful word *No.* Once the deed is done, the world is immediately a better place. The sun will shine on the Yellow Brick Road, the villagers will dance

in the streets, the birds will sing, and the celestial chorus will join in a heaven-sent rendition of "Happy Days
Are Here Again."

Above all, you are free. The word *No* does this to
people.

CHAPTER 3

THE FAMILY

*When we speak of family ties, let us not forget
the noose.*

I have spoken with many people who either work
or have worked in mental institutions. To this
date, I have yet to meet anyone who can report a
patient who was put there because of the national debt, the atomic bomb, the rising divorce rate,
or the depletion of the rain forests. The most
common reason for residency in a mental institution is *family*: the stresses, strains, and fancied
obligations of the blood tie. We put our children, spouses, parents, and siblings into locked
rooms by our constant and unyielding demands.

I remember talking with a young lady during a
guest appearance on a radio show in Miami. The
topic, of course, was the word *No*, and most of the
people who called desperately needed some prod-
ding in a negative direction. This woman was 31
years old, had never had a date, and rarely left
her home at night. And the reason? She *owed* it to

her parents to stay home and tend to their needs. After all, they had given her life and looked after her during the years of her childhood, so she had assumed a massive debt. To make this bondage even more complete, she wasn't even allowed to keep her paycheck. Instead, she received an allowance for lunch and small purchases. It had come to this point only because it was a lifetime pattern and she didn't know how to handle it. Fortunately, she had summoned the courage to call a talk-radio program and hear a sympathetic man tell her to get out of that house immediately. (In fact, I even offered to help her pack.)

A similar turn-over-your-check situation involved a milksop who went to work every day of his life without a penny in his pocket. His loving wife saw no need for him to have any money because he had a gasoline credit card and his company had a cafeteria arrangement whereby the cost of the lunch was deducted from the employee's paycheck. The loving wife (naturally) checked the take-home pay and the gasoline bill carefully to assure that no funny business was going on. (It is a well-known fact that men with no money in their pockets really tear up the pea patch when they are away from their wives.)

Although these cases seem to be rather extreme, they really aren't that far away from the norm. Both are examples of strong family members keeping a weaker one under their thumb until the inevitable state of torpor takes over. In both of these cases, the answer is to say *No*, loudly and clearly. These aren't situations that need "talking over" or any "exchange of viewpoints." After all, who ever talked it over with the victims?

One does not reason with the unreasonable.

Many people spend the better part of a lifetime hoping that a situation will change, but familial strangleholds are not self-correcting. When a person finds something that works—illness, obligation, or even simple brute strength—there will be no voluntary retreat. People simply do not give up something that works every time.

> *Waiting for people to reform themselves is like standing on the wrong street and waiting for a bus that never comes.*

I have seen cases where something as simple as a nasty disposition has been used to keep other family members in line. Some people are so afraid of conflict they will do anything to keep the monster placated. When a child learns that being nasty and abusive gets results, he grows into adulthood with that particular hand tool hooked to his belt; if it got him out of helping with the dishes or pulling weeds at the age of 8, it will do wonders at 38. Unfortunately for the rest of us, it also is often a successful stratagem, and our "solution" is that it is easier to do the job ourselves than to fight about it, to hand out money, to turn over the car keys, or even to open the guest room. People with bad dispositions learn early on that bile pays off, that people around them will give in rather than face abuse. So, they put this bile to work and reload for the next volley.

It seems rather incredible that these abusive people are so evenly spread around the families of America. An old friend of mine (who we call the Sage of Bakersfield) once evolved a theory that the Almighty, as part of a grand plan, put one abuser, one moocher, and one hypochondriac into every family. My friend calls it the *Theory of Obnoxious Dispersion.* It is an interesting concept, but it would take considerable research to establish its validity. Also, I am not at all sure about the cause and the result. Maybe the family dynamic creates its own undesirable members. My own belief is that moochers and hypochondriacs are environmentally created, but the abusive, nasty ones are born that way. This is determined at the moment of conception, and once they find that abuse pays off, they don't even bother with the cover-up. Some people are just born nasty, and they carry it with them until the end, like having six toes.

While it might be argued that blood is thicker than water, it is also true that many less-than-intrepid individuals have some difficulty coming up for air when they are buried under layers of this hoary old bromide. Blood ties, it would seem to any rational person, are for helping and caring, not for subjugating and certainly not for paying back old debts. If there is one phrase responsible for the break-up of the American family, it is "You owe me."

It all comes back to the matter of obligation and responsibility discussed in the previous chapter. People who give birth have a responsibility to that child until he is able to shift for himself. There is no reciprocal responsibility, and obligation doesn't enter into it at all. If a son or daughter wants to look after an aging parent, it is a matter of simple love, but there is no balancing of the ledger. This is not an accounting class. We do not owe anything to anyone for being born, and we must not be told otherwise. Child-rearing does not warrant a curtain call; it is what you are supposed to do when you have children.

It should be established that we have no obligations or responsibilities for situations we do not control. If the family loser gets into one mess after another without our consent or knowledge, then we are not obligated to bail him out. Too often, the adviser is told to mind his own business, but it all becomes his business once it is time to pay for the ride.

There is, or should be, a direct correlation between advice and responsibility. If Mother and Dad advise a daughter not to marry an obvious lout, and she

ignores that advice, why should they have the responsibility to take her back (often two children and 20 black
eyes later)? It is one thing to argue that a person
matures by making his own mistakes; it is another
thing altogether when it is someone else who pays for
those mistakes.

> *If I tell you what I would do in a certain situation, you
> have every right to ignore my advice but no right to send
> me the bill.*

The family is a festering breeding ground for the
debt-and-obligations game. The only way to fight back is
to take a long and serious appraisal of what you *do* and
do not owe to anyone. Certainly, you do not owe anyone
for a problem that is not of your making, and there is
no need to feel guilty about saying *No* in this situation.

Let us not forget that *helping* has nothing to do with
being told of one's obligations. When a parent voluntarily helps a son or daughter make a down payment on a
house or one brother helps another start a business, we
are talking about voluntary gestures of good will. These
are not part of the old you-owe-it-to-me game. This is
something that a person wants to do, and indeed feels
good about doing, and it has nothing to do with obligations. A gift is an act of love. An obligation is more close-
ly connected with the yoke and the whip.

People living in Florida and Southern California are
especially vulnerable to family incursions, because the
locations are so desirable to vacationers. One couple of
our acquaintance, Art and Marilyn, once lived in Santa
Monica. They came from Wisconsin, both from big
families, and the relatives were thrilled finally to have a
California connection. ("Geez, they're right at the
beach!") They were good friends of ours, but we gave
up on seeing them between May and September. Why?

Because they were always tied up with relatives. The folks in Wisconsin would get together during the winter and map out their vacation plans. ("We'll take the last 2 weeks of May, Joe and Margaret get the first 2 weeks of June, and Sam and Edna will take the last 2 weeks of June. Okay, now for July . . .")

When they came, they all expected the full Los Angeles treatment as well: Disneyland, Universal City, Dodger and Angel Stadiums, movie-stars' homes, and the customary overnighter in San Diego or Santa Barbara. This applied to *each* group; once one had gone, the next wave arrived and expected the same thing. Even though they paid their own way—they had been saving all year—Art and Marilyn had to pay for themselves, over and over and over again. They went into the fall season not only dead broke but physically exhausted.

After five straight summers of this, they decided that they had had enough, but how do you say it without— get ready!—"hurting their feelings?" Our friends had long since passed the point of hoping for relief, a time when the family would decide that this California couple needed a rest—indeed, might want a summer vacation of their own. Such wishing was of course an exercise in futility, because anyone who would swarm on a relative like a plague of locusts would never of their own volition call a halt. They just keep coming, and coming, and coming. This is the way that locusts move; a natural flow doesn't reroute itself.

I had lunch with the husband one day, and he asked if I had any kind of solution (short of doing the one thing that had to be done). They had discussed going away for the summer, but they couldn't afford to stay anywhere for long, and he would need to take an unpaid leave of absence. They had also discussed turning the tables and going to Wisconsin, but this was only a temporary reprieve. (The locusts would just follow them back.)

The only answer—which neither one of them wanted to hear—was to write a letter putting a stop to it all. The problem had come down to the same bedrock where so many problems land. A person must either put up with a miserable situation or make someone unhappy and end it. We can spend the rest of our lives looking for that third road to travel, but it isn't going to be there.

Our friends finally bit the bullet and did what had to be done. They wrote the letter, made copious Xerox copies, and sent it to the entire distribution list in Wisconsin. They made their home available only for the first 2 weeks of June, and they suggested that family members draw lots for the visiting rights. The letter also stated the husband would not be taking his vacation at this time, because they might like to take a vacation for themselves. Of course, this caused a great uproar with both families, and no one in Wisconsin was able to work up a grain of understanding for our friends' position. However, the deed was done. (The husband retired a few years ago, and our friends moved to Idaho, where no one ever visits them. There is a lot to be said for Idaho.)

In all of these cases, I have cited the difficulty that people have in saying *No* to anyone who might in any way be considered family. Sometimes the fringe hangers also nurture from the main line, and therefore their impact can be surprisingly powerful. The alternative to saying *No* is to put up with an unpleasant or impossible situation. This is a fact that absolutely must be faced.

The problem arises from the great myth of "compromise" that we all carry with us from birth to grave. We believe there is always a way to solve a problem by having both sides talk it over, give a little, and then meet somewhere in the middle. It is instilled in us as children, and we believe, *believe, BELIEVE!*, even though it isn't true at all. For the most part, we do not reach agreements by compromise but rather by one side giving in completely. This is the way the world works and is demonstrated daily. We rarely see it, however. With most of the problems we face and the decisions that we make, there rarely is even a chance for compromise. For example:

- The children go to public school *or* they go to private school.
- Her mother lives with us *or* her mother does not live with us.
- I accept the transfer *or* I do not accept the transfer.
- We buy a new car this year *or* we do not buy a new car this year.
- We have dinner at home *or* we have dinner out.

Most of the decisions that we make are *either/or* decisions, yet we start each day firmly believing that all problems can be discussed and resolved through compromise. The result is the daily brick wall we hit when our beliefs are shattered once again. And we act surprised each time this happens, even though it happens every day.

Most family problems can be filed under *E*, for Either/Or. They just don't lend themselves to compromise. There is no middle ground. It all comes down to *Yes* or *No*—with *No* being strongly discouraged—and therein lies the formula for instant stress. Family-derived stress can be identified by breaking it down into five basic categories, which we will call the *Five Expectations*:

1. Presence Expectation
2. Performance Expectation

3. Acceptance Expectation

4. Allegiance Expectation

5. Accommodation Expectation

The *Presence Expectation* was illustrated in the previous chapter by Andy and Marcy, where Marcy's presence was expected every Sunday at the cemetery. It is also quite evident when one is expected for certain holidays and often even Sunday dinner, regardless of your own personal wishes. At holiday time, we often hear the sad stories of people who are alone, but we never hear of the people forced to go somewhere they don't want to be and to associate with people they don't particularly like. These people might *prefer* to be alone.

The *Performance Expectation* does its damage with people who are expected to achieve certain standards when they lack either the ability or the interest to meet them. For example, Mother and Dad have college degrees, so their children are expected to earn degrees, which is a reasonable expectation of any young person with the ability to make it through college. Suppose, however, that one of their children is not a student and had great difficulty making it through high school. This one doesn't have a prayer of getting through the freshman year at Mortimer Snerd Community College. He or she will fail to meet the expectation and therefore disappoint the parents, grandparents, aunts, uncles, cousins—and presumably even the family next door.

I know of a specific case in which a young man obtained a master's degree, with academic honors, then accepted a job as a letter carrier. Why? Because he knew that he would be happy doing that for a living (and in fact, he was). His mother and wife joined forces in a continuing harangue, however, about "amounting to something," which actually meant doing something that he hated. This seems to be a uniquely American belief: anyone who isn't doing something that he hates really isn't trying. In this "Case of the Happy Letter Carrier," there seemed to be no interest in the fact that he was a thoroughly happy individual, only two women who saw a university solely as a job-training bureau. In their minds, this man had somehow failed them, the rest of the family, and even the entire North American continent when the truth was that he had failed *no one*. Few people understand the idea of obtaining a degree solely to become an educated person and not to find a place in the corporate hierarchy.

The *Acceptance Expectation* concerns itself with accepting set family beliefs and practices. Let's say that the family—aunts, uncles, nephews, nieces, the whole clan—congregates in the park every Sunday for a picnic and a softball game. This is a family ritual. It might well be argued this is a nice, even admirable custom, but what about the person who doesn't want to participate? Or what about the person who doesn't vote the same way the family votes, or attend the family church, or think the way that the family thinks on any given issue? The person who doesn't want to play softball in the park on Sunday (or even *be* in the park on Sunday) certainly isn't depriving anyone else of the experience. Some families would respect this person's right to make an individual decision, but others would not.

Many years ago, I worked with a young man who married a secretary in our department. As I later learned, she was the youngest and the only girl in a family of five children. These people were avid hunters, and she was taken along on hunting trips from the time that she could walk. She had no memory of anything but Dad and her older brothers declaring war on every four-footed creature in the forest. Shortly after the wedding, Dad and the brothers gave the new husband a rifle, hunting outfit, and complete instructions on the correct way of blowing a deer's tiny brains into the Great Beyond. They also informed him that he was expected to join them in the woods from that moment on. To marry into that family was to be an instant deerslayer.

At that precise moment, this young man was presented with a major problem. He had known that these people were hunters, but he hadn't any idea that he was to be included in their carnal revels. He also saw no reason to march off into the woods and shoot an animal, nor did he have the slightest desire to sleep on the ground or to hunker by the fire. (His idea of a vacation was a room with a view in San Francisco.) He told this to the family and said that he hoped they could get their money back on the hunting equipment. This immediately sparked great resentment, and he became an instant outsider. The interpretation of his refusal to hunt was that he was condemning them and, by so doing, setting himself above them. It was taken as an insult when the truth was he said nothing more than he didn't want to go hunting. His wife took the family's side, and the friction only increased. She joined in the collective booing and hissing, and they divorced within a year. This is a clear example of the Acceptance Expectation at work.

The *Allegiance Expectation* probably hits harder than any of the other expectations. This one puts blood relationships above the law and even accepted standards of both morality and decency. Those who believe in the Allegiance Expectation would expect one family member to hide another if that person were escaping from the law, or to help conceal a transgression even when they knew that the person was guilty.

In a situation not quite as dramatic as that of an escapee looking for a place to hide, I recall a case that I encountered many years ago when I was in college. Gordon, a classmate of mine, was an excellent student.

He graduated with high honors, which he accomplished through hard work and by giving up many of the good times that are always associated with college life. Gordon had a younger brother, however, whose name I have thankfully long since forgotten, who viewed higher education in quite another way. He didn't study, cheated when he could, managed to guess right a few times, and somehow made it through his freshman year with a marginal record. He was on academic probation early in his sophomore year, but this didn't put a crimp in his social life. The proverbial push came to shove when he reached the final exam in American History. It was a big class, one of those 100-plus affairs in which the teacher didn't know anyone's name and only gave objective tests. Little brother knew that he couldn't pass the test; he had never opened the book and rarely ever came to class. He also knew that another *F* would put him out in the street, so he decided that brother Gordon would take the test for him. Gordon refused, and the little brother failed.

When the family learned that the little brother was about to be bounced from the halls of academia, they joined forces and put the heat directly on Gordon. "How could you do this to your brother?!" they cried. Gordon felt rather strongly, and with considerable justification, that brother had done it to himself. He flatly refused to bail out a lummox in a mess that was entirely self-made. As expected, the little brother was expelled and spent the rest of his life blaming Gordon for not helping him in his hour of greatest need. The family agreed, forcing Gordon to fail the only test of his own academic career: the Allegiance Expectation.

The *Accommodation Expectation* is based on the principle of rearranging space and time to meet the needs of relatives. When Aunt Mildred arrives unannounced from Peoria, a family member is expected to give her a place to stay. If Aunt Mildred brings Uncle Edgar and their four children, then perhaps two family members will be expected to open their homes. This continues with more and more homes being offered as the visiting wave grows.

It is the same situation with time as well. Family members are expected to be flexible in their schedules to accommodate the needs of their kin, whether it means sitting through a piano recital, showing up at a wedding, or stopping by to listen to Grandpa complain about his bunions. This is expected.

A young bachelor friend of mine, Chuck, was once told by the family elders that he was to "take in" a ne'er-do-well cousin who was getting out of prison and had no place to go. It was explained that "the boys" were about the same age, so it would be a Jim-Dandy living arrangement—as though they were about to start double-dating and joining the gang at the malt shop. Chuck wanted no part of this because:

A) He liked living alone;

B) He had never liked the cousin, going back to their earliest childhood;

C) The man was a lifelong thief, and he didn't want to start hiding his wallet and his watch; and

D) He resented the decision being made without even asking him.

Unlike some of the other people I have mentioned so far, Chuck is a man who has no trouble employing the word *No*, and he didn't agonize over this decision for as long as 30 seconds. In fact, the answer wasn't just *No*, but *Hell No!*, which carries the idea that it also applies in the future. I don't know what happened to the cousin, but Chuck went on living his happy bachelor life, the problem solved before it even had time to become a minor irritation. This is unquestionably the best way to handle any problem that must eventually be resolved anyway by telling someone *No*.

Everyone, unfortunately, is not a Chuck, and many people have great difficulty standing up to the old warriors who control the arsenal of expectation. Most of the stress comes from fear of failing the test, not in the fallout from the refusal. Therefore, people who really want to say *No* but cannot will go on year after year giving in to family pressures and, in the process, taking another giant step each time toward the friendly neighborhood sanitarium.

If I could sell no other message, I would choose the one about saying *No* when that is exactly what you want to do. Believe me, the world will not go to pieces when this word is spoken. On the contrary, it will become a brighter, happier place, and you will have a lot more self-esteem.

When the pressures being heaped on you come from people with no right to invoke those pressures in the first place, the guilt should be theirs and not yours. When you give in, you are playing their game. It is a poor coach who plays to the other team's strength, and it makes no more sense in life than it does on the playing field.

You must also never lose sight of the fact that there is little happiness or personal satisfaction to be derived from giving in to avoid a fight. *Think about this!* Has it ever made you happy, cut down on stress, or created a better family relationship? Of course not. Giving in does nothing but placate the bully, and a bully does not have to fit the stereotype of an oversized street kid. Bullies come in various packages, including those who sit in rocking chairs and knit, who advertise bad health, and who create debts and obligations with all the ease of creating a smoke ring or a snowball. When there is a family bully, there is unhappiness, dissension, and stress.

Anyone who is faced with this situation has two choices: 1) live with it, or 2) get rid of it. The second option makes a lot more sense.

4

LOVE AND MARRIAGE

The tragedy of our age is that marriage is invariably emotional while divorce is logical.

It is impossible to get squared away on the subject of love and marriage without first comprehending the opposing forces of emotions and intellect. Anyone who lets the emotions rule is in for a stormy and completely unsatisfactory love life.

In all things—and certainly love and marriage—the intellect must rule the emotions. Think of your emotions as something like taking the dog out for a walk. The animal has a certain amount of freedom, but there is still some control at work.

The emotions are what make us laugh, sing, and enjoy ourselves, but they must always be under the direct control of the intellect. It is one thing to be impulsive, but this must be in the context of order. It might be fun, for example, to fly away on an unplanned trip to Rio de Janeiro or

Timbuktu, but only if the bills are paid and some money will still be in the bank when you return. Otherwise, this just creates a brand-new set of problems.

Impulsive people are almost always problem people. They pride themselves on their independence, often to the point of being monumental bores, but they are the first to lean on others when the bill comes due. I don't think that I would find these people quite so offensive if they didn't spend so much time describing what devil-may-care scamps they really are and looking for our resultant admiration. As an entertainment device, it is about one step ahead of war stories and vacation slides.

Impulsiveness is certainly not a desirable factor in the love-and-marriage department. While love is indeed an emotion, it must always be tempered with a more-than-equal supply of intellect. No matter how good the other person looks to you, the ultimate idea in marriage is to spend a lifetime together. Remember that marriage does not solve anything. If you are not compatible now, the situation will not improve after marriage. Bad habits will become intolerable habits, and weaknesses will grow into major character defects. This is when the intellect must take over, because a permanent arrangement must be based on something deeper than agitated glands.

Okay, so what does all this have to do with the word *No*? The answer is everything. *No* comes from the brain, and *Yes* is a direct issue of the glands. It is the "negative" side of people that keeps them out of trouble; the "positive" side lashes them to the ant hill.

- *Yes* tells us to drive home when we have had too much to drink; *No* tells us to call a cab.
- *Yes* tells us to charge an expensive item that we can't afford; *No* tells us not to buy it.

- *Yes* tells us to squeeze some more miles out of bald tires and bad brakes; *No* tells us to take care of the problem now.
- *Yes* tells us to gamble with money we don't have; *No* tells us not to take the risk.
- *Yes* sends us into marriages without a chance of working; *No* tells us to back off and find someone else.

Although the Grand High Potentates of positive thinking tell us nothing is worse than a negative attitude, they are completely, absolutely wrong. I don't know if there is any correlation between the popularity of this asinine philosophy and the growing divorce rate—to say nothing of the crime rate—but I suspect that some direct connection might exist. Positive thinking promotes emotionalism, and this is the cornerstone of a bad marriage.

It is a matter of record (absolutely proven by statistics) that successful marriages are built on a commonality of background. This means that two Methodists from Mason City, Iowa, have a better chance of staying married than, say, a Roman Catholic from San Francisco and a Jehovah's Witness from Athens, Georgia. Intellectually, there is a small voice that tries to tell us this, but sometimes we don't listen. There is always some idiot around to offer the worst advice in the world— "Follow your heart"—and we often follow it all the way to Divorce Court.

So, the first rule when considering marriage is to give your intellect an equal shot in the decision. Once married, the word *No* comes into play in a way that will make the marriage work. I refer to Smith's *Marital Veto Principle*, which forms the absolute bedrock for any successful marriage. Recall from the Introduction that it is better to give up something we want than to have something thrust on us that we don't. This is the basis of the Veto Principle.

There are many activities that married people often, even usually do separately: shopping trips, football games, fashion shows, fishing, and so on. These do not fall in the domain of the Veto Principle, which applies only to those activities that couples normally do together. Under the terms of this principle, either party has the right to avoid the activity just by saying *No*, and the other party is obligated to respect the spouse's wishes. Stated more simply, *No* always take precedence over *Yes*.

The first reaction to the Veto Principle often is that it would tend to negate all activity and leave the couple sitting home every night. I am quite sure that this objection comes from people who are accustomed to being dragged—or to dragging someone else—to activities they don't enjoy, or to being forced to associate with disagreeable people. It doesn't have to be this way at all. If she can say *No* to him and he can say *No* to her, then their social life will be spent doing things they both enjoy. They are casting out all of the unpleasantness and leaving only the good parts.

This is much like the ancient American art of making corn whiskey. Barrels of mash are tossed into a frozen stream, the water and other nonalcoholic impurities are then frozen, and the alcohol goes to the center of the barrel, remaining in its liquid state. The sludge is thrown away, the remaining alcohol is combined in other barrels, and the process is repeated, each time with more impurities being removed. Then there is more condensing and more freezing, with the distiller and Mother Nature combining their talents until the end result is achieved: a barrel of smooth, sweet, pure corn whiskey (one of the premiere products ever to come out of the United States).

The Veto Principle is the same kind of process, with the constant removal of those people and events that bring displeasure to either of the marriage partners. Each one's interests predominate with the other, which alone is enough to make any marriage work, and the result is like the pure moonshine in the final barrel. Neither party is dragged to anything, and neither has to associate with people they consider offensive. Everything they do together is something that they both want to do. Everyone they see is someone who they both want to see.

Men and women do not have a lot of built-in compatibility, and this is the reason that a marriage must have everything possible working for it. Regardless of the claims made by strong feminists, the male and female genders are coming from totally different places. Men and women have deep-seated philosophic differences that exhibit themselves in many ways.

Have you ever observed the two sexes on a house- or apartment-hunting operation, for example? It won't take more than a few minutes to note the differences. Women immediately head for closets and cupboards, because these are important things to a woman. Men don't care one iota about closets and cupboards. I have had it explained to me at least a thousand times why closets and cupboards are essential to human existence, but I still can't work up any interest. A man looks at the amount of space that will eventually need to be painted (stone and wood-paneled walls are a plus to a man) and whether the place is plumbed for a wet bar. (These are of minimal concern to a woman.)

Alternatively, have you ever noticed employees going to work in the morning? You will often see women arriving with gift-wrapped packages, but never men. Women are very big for exchanging gifts in the workplace. It would never have occurred to me (a one-time, so-called "gray suit") to bring a birthday gift for the guy at the next desk.

Listen to men and women talking to the painter. Women like subtlety in colors; for instance, "In this room I want just a hint of green—just a teeny, teeny green cast—only a suggestion, a hint." A man would say, "Paint it green." In clothing, women lean toward patterns that blend: a chocolate brown, for example, that blends into a light brown, to a tan, to a beige, and eventually to a white. A man would prefer a brown-and-white stripe. Whenever I see a man in a color-blended shirt, I know that his wife picked it out.

Women are better small talkers than men. Men are better than women at parking cars. Women are better at gift wrapping (or any kind of wrapping for that matter), but they are terrible at map reading. Few women can make a decent martini, but women are better dancers than men and better at growing indoor plants.

All of this is meant to establish the indisputable fact that men and women are basically different creatures. Neither is better nor worse, only different. They think differently, and they react differently to the same stimuli, which means that compatibility is not easily attained. When two people embark on an essentially incompatible relationship that is based on nothing but emotion, the chances for survival are minimal at best.

The only way that men and women can ever be passably compatible is for each to acquire a healthy respect for that magnificent word *No.* There are many things that people simply have to do, unpleasant as they are. It is not particularly dangerous to the relationship when they are doing something that neither wants to do, such as a party at the boss' house, a business-related wedding they can't get out of, or maybe an obligatory visit to someone at the hospital. Compatibility does not suffer when neither person is enjoying the occasion and they have a common interest in ducking out early. It is only when one has been dragged that the relationship suffers, and this is where the word *No* comes into it.

I think any rational person would agree that men and women have to meet on an intellectual plane for there to be any kind of worthwhile coexistence. Passion is good for a 3- or 4-week run, but there comes a time when one person makes an intelligible statement and the other one actually replies. This day inevitably arrives when the bloom is off the rose, and those who aren't ready for it really aren't ready for anything.

It must be a terribly traumatic experience to complete a year or two of married life, then realize that you are pledged into eternity with a complete imbecile. Extremely "positive" people lean toward imbecility, because they are nonselective and unable to discriminate between good and bad, between quality and garbage. When I hear a person described as someone who "likes everything," I immediately envision someone with an IQ of about 15, a "good sport" who has trouble holding a fork.

People with good sense are discriminating in their tastes and find it difficult to accept the unacceptable. Intelligent people reject, but fools never do.

Because compatibility is geared for the long run, I have often thought that the emphasis in marriage should be shifted from the wedding to the first anniversary. A wedding is nothing more than a manifestation of physical attraction, even when the participants are already living together. A shared living arrangement where "either of us can walk out if it doesn't work" isn't any kind of commitment; only in a legally binding marriage do two people learn if they have the maturity, the compassion, and the intelligence to make it over the long haul. Therefore, I think that the wedding should be simple and the big bash reserved for the first anniversary. The first year is much more significant than the engagement, and those 12 months together are more worthy of celebration than the wedding itself.

My friend, the Sage of Bakersfield, is in favor of a premarital test, much like the test we give for US citizenship. Before he married his second wife, he asked her to name the 50 state capitals (she got 47 right) and the last three Vice-Presidents. She passed the test, even though she had no idea that her impending marriage was riding on the results. (The Sage's first wife thought that Seattle was the capital of Oregon, and this soured the relationship considerably.) This second marriage has worked out quite well, so the Sage has followed up with a 60-question test to be given to both parties before a marriage, with the recommendation that only two passers—or two failers—should marry each other. Although he says that he wouldn't spend his life with anyone less than a "55," he considers 45 to be a passing grade. Anyone who scores less than 45, in his view, is not only not worth marrying but someone who is not even worth knowing.

The first 50 questions are a list of the states, from Alaska to Wyoming, with the goal being to name the capital of each one. This is followed by:

51. Who invented the telephone?
52. If you knew the diameter of a circle, how would you find its circumference?
53. Who was the first Vice-President of the United States?
54. Who wrote *For Whom The Bell Tolls?*

55. Which two states are the largest in area and in population? (No half-point credit on this one.)
56. What is the first book of the Holy Bible?
57. What subject would you be studying if you had to memorize Faraday's Law?
58. Who represents your district in Congress?
59. Name one ballet composed by Tchaikovsky.
60. What is the capital of Canada?

Although the Sage doesn't envision this test ever being backed with the force of law, he does consider it an excellent guide for anyone who is contemplating matrimony: a simple case of knowing what one is getting.

I think that the real value of premarital testing is in the admonition that only passers and failers should marry each other. Two lunkheads who can't even name their own state capital will probably be quite compatible. All they need is a six-pack, *The National Enquirer*, and—God help us—each other, and they will achieve total bliss. The only thing that could ever befoul this Edenic situation is if one of them decided to take a class or in any way seek some intellectual improvement.

> *When two fools marry, they owe it to each other to remain fools.*

At the other end of the spectrum, two bright people who share an awareness of the world around them also have a good chance of making it together. "Cross-breeding," however, is a dangerous business at best. Bright people should never marry imbeciles, no matter how strong the physical attraction. All that anyone can ever expect in this situation is a one-night stand and a pleasant memory.

It was back in the 1950s that the positive-thinking twaddle started making inroads into the American psyche, and it was inevitable that it would invade the love relationship as well. In itself, positive thinking is a harmless (albeit unworkable) bit of fluff, but its danger lies in its complete lack of definition. It is a fuzzy, shallow, sunshine philosophy. It is all things to all people. Since its inception, the unlettered and unknowing have adopted it and run off in all directions, interpreting and bending it meet their own needs.

While existentialism found its way into the camps of the semi-educated—who misinterpreted with unfettered abandon—positive thinking became the holiest of holies to the poorly educated and the not very bright. People began exhorting one another to "be positive" and began tackling impossible projects with no preparation whatsoever, screaming, "I can, I *can*, I *CAN!*" when they indeed could not. And not the least of these impossible projects is the union of two people who think they can solve anything with a good, positive attitude. Like any other human activity, marriages are fueled by the force of reality. One starts by seeing the intended mate for who and what he or she is, accepting the appraisal as an indispensable fact of life, and then going on from there.

I once worked with a man named Bill who was quite good at his job and for the most part a likable person. Unfortunately, he had a drinking problem, and over a period of several years I watched the problem grow. His ever-faithful and loving wife, Linda, was the positive thinker to end all positive thinkers, and she wasn't about to see the dark side of anything. This woman was in fact so perpetually cheerful that I found it difficult to spend much time with her. My own wife and I saw Bill and Linda at many social functions, and they all ended the same way. Bill was bombed halfway through the evening, and Linda had to drive home. There were also the unfailing explanations that always avoided the obvious issue: Bill hasn't eaten since breakfast; Bill didn't get any sleep last night, and he is *so* tired; Bill has been under a lot of stress; Bill is taking medication, and he shouldn't have had a drink.

Everyone else in the room knew exactly what the problem was. Bill was a lush, and the one thing that Bill did not need was the kind of "support" that his wife gave him. He didn't need—shouldn't have had—the constant cover-up. What Bill needed was a loud, unmistakable *No*. This simply was not the way that a healthy marriage works.

There is a certain *rightness* to the male–female relationship that is essential if anything good will ever come from it. Linda and Bill were not *right*. She ignored the obvious, and the obvious needed a little sunlight. The positive-thinking, go-for-it approach to love and romance also ignores the *rightness* of the situation, which is why married people cheat and single people lie to each other. It is a matter of staging a play that cannot exist outside the theater.

Rightness has nothing to do with the similar-sounding *righteousness*, or any other kind of holier-than-thou malarkey. Rightness occurs with two people who are free to enter a romantic relationship and who have been honest with each other. Obviously, if she has a child that he does not know about, or if he has a prison record that she does not suspect, then there is something lacking in the rightness department.

The old "I'll-marry-you-when-the-kids-are-grown" routine doesn't fit the pattern, either. In this, one person is lying and the other is a willing participant in an adulterous relationship. What good can come from it? Also, the woman who would believe such a moldy old line is so patently stupid that she isn't worth having anyway. It is akin to the old Groucho Marx line, "I wouldn't belong to any organization that would have me as a member." Shifted slightly to the love-and-marriage scene, a man might well say, "I wouldn't marry anyone so dumb that she believes the line I'm using to get her into bed."

Now that we have covered the manner in which two people should act toward each other in the love-and-marriage game, we should look at their relationships with other people. There is probably no more significant line in the marriage vows than "forsaking all others," which means that your (plural) interests come first—always, forever, and into eternity. Putting another person's interests over those of one's mate is just as great a violation of the marriage vows as adultery and desertion would be.

To put it succinctly, a married person's first loyalty, first duty, and first responsibility is to the spouse. Other people get what is leftover. If this sounds a bit harsh, then reverse it and see if the words sound right: the spouse gets what's leftover. Do you like that one better?

Remember that money, time, and attention are limited. Those who make demands on other people are necessarily looking for a place on their ladder of priorities. In marriage, we don't play for a tie. Somebody is first, and somebody else is second. This is not only the way that it *is*, but the way that it *has to be*. (As the line goes, "forsaking all others." If you agree to it, then mean it.)

To put one's mate first, it is often necessary to invoke the negative, or to say *No*. Let's look at one example. Bart and Maxine had been married for three years and had lived all of that time in Los Angeles. They had wanted to go to Paris on their honeymoon but couldn't afford it, so they had saved all of that time. They called it their Three-Year-Plan. Through careful management they saved enough for the trip, and right on schedule, they were ready to go. Bart was looking forward to the trip, but his enthusiasm paled when compared with Maxine's. She was ecstatic over the thought of it. *Paris!*

About a month before they were to leave, however, Bart received a phone call at work from his sister. She told him about a big family reunion in Nebraska, and Bart was to schedule his vacation accordingly. The plan was to rent a van, and the California contingent (eight people in all) would travel *en masse* to meet the others in Nebraska. Relatives were coming from all directions—and, oh!—wasn't it going to be fun?

Bart told her about the trip to Paris, and that he couldn't get another vacation for a whole year, and that Maxine had her heart set on going, and so on. Sister would have none of it. "You can go to Paris any time," she said, "but the family might never get together again." In his sister's mind, it had already been decided: Bart and Maxine were as good as in the van and speeding toward the Great Plains.

It was now crunch time for Bart. He waffled at first and said that he would get back to her as soon as he could "clear up a few things." When he put down the phone, he intended to call Maxine and explain the situation, but then, in one of those marvelous revelations that come so seldom in a lifetime, he realized what it meant to be married. He realized what his responsibilities were to his wife as opposed to his family. Bart called his sister back, and he told her flatly and irrevocably *No*. He and his wife were going to Paris, and that was the end of it.

His sister was terribly upset. His brother-in-law didn't care much one way or the other, and several aunts and uncles wondered what was becoming of this generation. They couldn't understand why a young couple would rather visit Paris than pitch horseshoes in a Nebraskan beanfield. A big rift developed between Bart and his family that never has quite healed, but he did what had to be done. It was quite significant, I thought, that he didn't even tell Maxine about the family reunion until they returned from the trip. Paris meant so much to her that he didn't want a load of guilt to be carried on her shoulders to the banks of the Seine. After that, it wouldn't really matter anyway.

There actually was a bigger issue at stake here than simply Paris versus Nebraska. The sister had said that they could go to Paris next year, but was this really true? If the family could cancel the trip once, then they could do it again. Priority would have been established. Bart and Maxine could have gone to Paris next year *only* if Bart's family allowed it.

As I think about the situation now, I have to equate it with the real meaning of marriage. People often actually *marry* long after the legal wedding date. In this case, the true marriage began when Bart got back on the phone and told his sister that he and Maxine were going to Paris. That is the precise moment when his wife became the top priority in his value system.

Much of the prematrimonial advice given to young people today is extremely bad. It all seems to be a spin-off of the old follow-your-heart emotional pap. It is also a sure-fire recipe for a bad marriage. People who follow their emotions are guaranteed to wind up in the divorce court, jail, or the hospital.

The best advice that anyone can give to someone contemplating marriage is to be hard-headed. Use the same logic that you would to buy common stock or to shop for a transmission overhaul. Forget the nonsense about those mythical bells ringing and ask if this is the right person for you, not just someone who will get the hormones agitated but a person with whom you will go to PTA meetings and Little League games, make mortgage payments, share a bathroom, and worry about the crabgrass. Even in love, a person is well advised to follow the dictates of the brain rather than the glands. After all, the brain is the one organ in the body that will never steer you wrong.

5

THE RETIREMENT YEARS

If you really don't want to do it, don't.

For some people, retirement truly represents the golden years. This is the time of life when they shed many old responsibilities from their youth and begin living the way that they have always wanted to live.

It is also the time of life when they become leaned on, the patsies and the marks. For many, it brings the assumption of new responsibilities. It is a time when the daughter comes home, bringing her children with her; when the son needs immediate cash to get himself out of a mess that he alone created; or when someone decides that the retiree has "plenty of time" to spare and tries to consume most of it.

Too often, we confuse self-interest with selfishness, and retirement is definitely a time when self-interest must be served. Unlike younger people, retirees don't get another shot at it.

Whatever they have is the result of a lifetime of planning, and they cannot go back and recoup their losses. For retirees, a loan is money that probably isn't going to be repaid; it is gone, lost, kaput, and down the sewer.

It is unfortunate that so many loans from retirees are never repaid, but the reason seems to be readily apparent. The person who needs a legitimate loan (for a correspondingly legitimate purpose) goes to a bank or lending agency with every expectation of repaying the money on a predetermined schedule. Those who turn to relatives and back them into a corner usually aren't good credit risks, people who don't intend to mail in their money with a payment coupon every month. The repayment is usually expressed in terms of "when I get back on my feet," which bears a close relationship to "wait 'til the sun shines, Nellie," and is also about as specific. We should remember as well that those who turn to retired people for money know full well that the money being loaned is generally already invested and constitutes part of their income.

Retirement is especially difficult for those people who have traditionally been the repository for other people's problems—the old *dumper* and *dumpee* game again. Dumpers never understand when the rules have changed and sometimes must be reminded that a new game has begun.

> *When a worker receives a gold watch and a farewell dinner, it should be understood that he is off-limits to poachers, a rhinoceros among humankind.*

I remember a situation many years ago involving Joe and Martha, a couple who were friends of my parents. In fact, it was the single event that influenced my thinking along the lines of enlightened negativism and would eventually form the framework for most of my writing. As I recall, I was about 14 years old when I first heard my parents talking about "poor Joe." It seems that Joe had retired after 40 years of employment with a public utility company and had planned to spend his retirement traveling and indulging his passion in life, amateur archaeology. Unfortunately, Martha's sister and her husband, who had just lost his job (again), decided to move in with them to cut down on expenses. Something was said about Joe and Martha having "plenty of room" (it wasn't Joe and Martha who said it) and the in-laws moved in— with Joe as the sole support of the household. Shortly after that, the new tenants' daughter left her husband and also moved in, only compounding the situation.

When I heard about all this, my adolescent mind looked for a single solution, and I wondered why Joe couldn't have just barred the door and said something like, "No, you aren't moving in." I was told that "things" just weren't that simple, and that I would understand when I was an adult. (As an aside, I can't help but reflect on the many things I was to understand when I reached the magic state of adulthood, and still fail to view in a new light.)

I now am an adult, and I still don't understand why Joe was required to support that pack of deadbeats. Incidentally, he was the sole support of this brood until he died 7 years later. The declining years of his life, which could have been happy and perhaps somewhat prolonged, were bent to the will of selfish, thoughtless people who took full advantage of another person's good nature and his aversion to confrontation.

Joe could have spent those years pursuing archaeology, the one interest that made him truly happy. Martha shared that interest, and they could have been quite happy in the role of historical sleuths. They had planned for it, invested wisely, and were ready for those golden years, only the "gold" was snatched from them.

This case is merely one variation among thousands that are happening all over this country. Someone is deemed to have "a big house" or "plenty of time," and *Zap!* Here come the marching locusts, ready for a feast. It is essential they be met and repulsed. A retiree has the right to think of the rest of his life as something sacred and inviolable. It is a simple case of saying, "It's mine, and you can't have it."

This should *not* be interpreted to mean that retirement is a time when a person turns his back on the world. The distinction to be made is between time and money freely given and that back-against-the-wall extortion, when it seems easier to come across with the loot than tell somebody to bugger off. The operative word here is *seems,* because we're dealing with an illusion. Paying off makes the immediate problem go away, but it will be back again tomorrow. The permanent solution is the word *No,* and it's also a lot cheaper.

Giving, helping, and caring are voluntary things. I have known more than one retired couple who willingly dug into their saddlebags and helped their children make down payments on that first house, or have given grandchildren financial packages to put them through college. This is not what this chapter is about. It's really about staying out of the net, and never being trapped into doing something that you don't want to do.

Henri Amiel said, "To know how to grow old is the master work of wisdom, and one of the most difficult chapters in the great art of living." These are wise words indeed, and I especially like the phrase about knowing "how to grow old." There is a definite knack to it. Some people are terrible at this, while others glide into it with all the grace of a gazelle and then wear age like a tailored suit. There is another step, though, and this is having the opportunity to exercise that knowledge. This is where *No* comes into the picture.

I received a lot of mail in the years immediately after *How to Cure Yourself of Positive Thinking* was published. In fact, I still correspond with several of these people, and one letter that I retrieved from my files came from Doug, a widower in Tucson, Arizona. He had read my book and seemed to regard finding out that he had the right to say *No* as some kind of personal awakening or revelation. I was especially interested in his particular problem, because it was a primary example of one that had no business existing, one that had been allowed to grow into real-stress proportions because of indecision and inaction. His situation, which he met obliquely for several months, was brought about by well-meaning friends, all of whom lived in his condominium complex. They were determined to "fix him up" with a widow who also lived there. He had no interest in the woman at all; in fact, he didn't even want her as a friend, much less romantically. He found her to be a dull-witted and completely uninteresting person, and he was bored into a semi-comatose condition whenever he found himself (however briefly) in her company.

The friends persisted, though, and invited him to all kinds of social functions where he and the widow would be the only single people present. The lady was reported to be quite interested in him, so there was no problem getting her to cooperate, attending each function and tossing a net into the water. For their part, the friends kept saying how much he and the lady had in common, always prefacing the perceived commonality with the expression "you two." For his part, he saw little similarity beyond the fact that they both had 10 fingers, 10 toes, and were air-breathing mammals. He tried to explain this, but his friends would have none of it. This is where he made his mistake: he skirted the problem rather than facing and eliminating it. He filled his social calendar with things that he didn't particularly want to do but that allowed him to be "busy" at all times. He also did whatever he could to avoid any face-to-face meetings with his old friends (by now his tormentors).

I am proud to say that after reading my book, this man saw the light. Bells rang, and the mental gears meshed. There was no need to avoid his old friends and no need to keep on being "busy," especially when it meant spending his time in pursuits with nothing going for them except they were better than the alternative. He invited the five worst offenders (three women and two men) to his home one evening, served a round of drinks to create an air of cordiality, then got on with business. He delivered his message:

> I have no interest in knowing Mrs. _____ , even as a friend, and I am asking all of you to cease in your efforts to bring us together. I am tired of making excuses and avoiding all of you, nor should it be necessary. We will now meet the problem head-on, and you are the problem. To put it succinctly—stop it!

There were some bruised feelings for awhile, of course. The problem came to an abrupt end, however, and everything soon returned to normal. He went on to enjoy his retirement, and was kind enough to recommend my book to anyone who had trouble saying *No*. (*Cure Yourself* sold rather well in Tucson, so there must have been some problems in this area.)

If we analyze the situation with any degree of intensity, we see several factors that are common to so many of our personal problems. First, there really shouldn't have been a problem at all. Doug allowed it to exist, and even helped it along, by his inaction. He should have gone to the host/hostess the day after the first special pairing with the widow and made it absolutely clear that he objected to such manipulation and let it be known, forcefully, that it wasn't to happen again.

Second, he spent too much time worrying about the feelings of those people who quite obviously hadn't stopped to consider his own. "Well-meaning" friends often are not well meaning at all; in fact, the term is almost satiric. Whenever it is used, a story of someone who completely mucked up a situation, and hurt someone in the process, usually follows.

Finally, he deluded himself into believing that a problem ignored is a problem solved. It isn't. Problems have remarkable staying power, and they are always waiting for you when you wake up in the morning.

I like this example because it is so typical of a universal problem. This was a relatively minor situation, little more than an irritant, that grew into something major because of a reluctance to say *No*. In this case, our man found himself inventing excuses, slipping out his own door at odd hours like a criminal, avoiding his old friends, and generally creating a lot of stress for himself. It wasn't necessary, as so many problems are not. It could have been avoided easily by saying the magic word. (By this time, I think we all know what the word is.)

Our British cousins use a phrase "the prime of life" to describe the retirement years, and it is most appropriate. Although some people elect to waste this great experience by growing old too soon, then whining because of fancied slights by younger people, most see the over-60 life as a shot at freedom. They are anxious to do all of those things there just wasn't time for when raising a family and scratching out a living, driving the children to games and music lessons, serving on committees, attending near-mandatory social functions, and being all things to all people.

Unfortunately, there also are many people who see the retiree as a mark and who aim all guns in that direction. To the Problem Perennial, the retiree represents the Holy Grail, the Golden Fleece, El Dorado, and the Emerald City, all rolled into one ripe-for-picking package. It is an unfortunate rule of life that if anyone is even assumed to possess a bit of spare cash, spare time, or spare energy, *someone* is going to ask for it.

> *True friendship is based on a lack of assumptions.*

Most retirees are quite unprepared for the role of pigeon. Responsible people invest their money, cover themselves with medical and dental insurance, if necessary move to more-affordable dwellings, and plan for just about every facet of retirement living. They do not, however, plan on the big bite, that unexpected relative or old acquaintance who is going to sweep down like a giant bird of prey and want a piece of a good thing. Usually, the bite is predicated on the assumption that the retiree is well able to absorb the incursion. ("What the hell, George and Mabel can afford it. They're loaded." Or perhaps, "They have time on their hands. They can babysit a couple of times a week.") It is an assumption that the Problem Perennial has no right to make (it is clearly none of his concern) but makes anyway.

I have always been an advocate of living defensively, and this attitude is particularly valuable for those who have reached retirement age. This is the time to raise the drawbridge, to circle the wagons, to man the parapets, and to issue extra ammunition to the troops. The enemy is out there, and he is going to hit every weak spot in the lines. Prepare for action, and hold your ground.

> *When we look for symbols in the animal world, let's forget the eagle and the lion, because defense is the key to life. Our standards should feature the cornered rat. Here we have a* survivor.

There are those who would find a lot of paranoia in these words, but that is only a surface analysis. Paranoia is a delusion, an irrational fear, and those very real people who stand on your doorstep with their luggage are not flights of fancy. The guy with his hand out for part of your pension is not a phantom. Those who believe that "cornered-rat" thinking is an irrational fear probably own stock in the Brooklyn Bridge and hold frequent conversations with the spirit world.

To step gracefully into the retirement years, a person is well advised to follow several basic rules, preferably beginning at the precise moment when retirement commences. In fact, it wouldn't be a bad idea to start practicing a few months before so it will come more easily later. Sometimes, quick reactions are a necessity. And these "golden" rules are:

1. Accept the indisputable fact that you are a mark.
2. Jealousy guard your money and your time.
3. Let your good works be voluntary. All giving must originate with you.
4. Do not compromise your own security for anyone.
5. Learn to anticipate a touch.
6. Never allow yourself to be backed into a corner. Do not commit to anything without taking time to contemplate.
7. Never respond to a self-made problem.
8. Practice saying *No* until it comes easily.

It is essential that the retiree be ultraconservative with time and money, because in neither case will there be

time to win them back. The days of risk-taking end
with retirement. There isn't time to speculate, nor
should it even be considered. The person who planned
wisely can coast on whatever he has going for him, but
he cannot take on an extra load. Personal security
must be guarded jealously, even selfishly.

I have mentioned the self-made problem as one of
the rules, and the retiree should recognize that there
is no way of keeping up with a person who is going to
jump back into the same mess after every bailout. The
gambler and the drinker, for example, are going to be
in trouble forever, unless *they* do something about their
problems. Get-rich-quick people and traffic violators
fall in the same category. Helping these people is not
like jump-starting a neighbor's car on a cold morning,
or babysitting for a friend in an emergency. Their
needs are never-ending, and you could make a career
of salvation with these Problem Perennials. It is one
thing to argue that these people have a disease (which
I question), but if so, it is a disease that people in their
retirement years do not need to share. Retirees need
these people in their lives like they need new wrinkles
or another pair of sore feet.

My wife and I had some neighbors once whose
daughter married (over their strong objections) an
imbecile who had dropped out of school, worked only
on occasion, and took great pleasure in dispensing cor-
poral punishment. Periodically, the daughter would
appear on their doorstep with various abrasions, contu-
sions, and lacerations, then stake a claim on her old
room. This time (of course) she had left him "for
good," but when the wounds were healed, she would
(of course) go back to the imbecile. ("I love him, and I
know that he loves me.") The cycle would start all over
again. This situation was chronic, and the problem
never ended. It turned out to be the parents' problem

as well as the daughter's, because they were always included in the consequences. The only difference was that they did not create it and did nothing to maintain it. Their only role was that they had to share a self-made, and as such an unnecessary, problem. It was dumped on the parents, and as far as I know, it is still going on—assuming that the imbecile hasn't killed her by this time. The one and only point is that it shouldn't have been *their* problem, and there was no reason they had to live with it.

The last of these rules is also important, and the retiree would do well to make the word *No* a part of everyday living, like buttering toast or checking the thermostat. Just as important as saying it, however, is *meaning* it, and backing it up. Remember that this word is to be used as though it were carved in stone, with no retreat and no alteration. The retirement years can be the high point of one's life or the ultimate in human misery. It is entirely up to you and your ability to drive the snakes from the garden.

LET'S BUILD BIGGER JAILS

The professional criminal is a volunteer. All that society asks of him is that he stop doing what he is doing, and this doesn't seem to be an unreasonable request. It isn't a great exaggeration to say that every man, woman, and child in the United States is capable of not stripping a car, not selling drugs, not vandalizing property and not robbing a store. No one is asking the lawbreaker to run a four-minute mile, to translate the Dead Sea Scrolls or to play a fugue on the harpsichord. Obeying the law requires no talent and no training. Anyone can do it.

These words originally appeared in a piece that I did for *The Freeman* and were picked up by *Reader's Digest* in the November 1991 issue. The point is found in the last sentence: "Anyone can do it."

Obeying the law is not an impossible—or even a difficult—request. Those who choose not to adhere to the rules of a civilized society do so of their own volition; therefore, they must be willing to pay the price.

Until now, we have been talking about the word *No* as it applies to the individual, but there is also a collective or social side to productive negativism. *No* can also be effective when it is directed at a social problem, just as when it is aimed at a mooching neighbor or the office gum-snapper. In this case, the problem is crime. The only answer for this problem that makes any sense to me is to build bigger jails. If two thirds of the population must keep the other one third locked up to protect itself, then so be it.

At this point in our intellectual development as a species, incarceration is the only method human beings have to deal with crime. Since my earliest childhood, I can recall adult conversations in which everyone agreed that we had to *get at the root* of crime. This was always spoken in a tone of finality as though someone had just solved a problem. People were probably nodding agreement for many generations before I came along, but unfortunately, no one has ever come close to finding this mysterious "root." We can go on adding our own assent to this tidy bit of bumper-sticker philosophy, but it simply won't accomplish anything.

My liberal friends assure me that poverty is the root of crime, and that a massive slum clearance and government-handout program would have everyone loving his neighbor and joining hands in song. This is also a lot of baloney, because if we accept this premise we then need to accept the rest of it: that all rich people are innately pure of heart, and the upper middle class is at least partially angelic. For my part, I just haven't found this to be true. There is no one yardstick that can predict criminal tendencies. Rich people kill, and poor people often rise to become public benefactors. White people and black people both commit crimes. Protestants, Catholics, Jews, Moslems, and Buddhists break the law everyday. Children from good homes grow up to become axe murderers. We don't know why people are criminals, so we can do nothing more than punish them once they prove they cannot function in a civilized society.

To illustrate this point of going with the tools that we have, let's look at the medical profession. Physicians of earlier times are considered to have been quite primitive, just as current medicine will be seen as something from the Stone Age even 100 years from today. My great grandfather, who fought with a Minnesota regiment in the Civil War, caught a bullet in his leg and was carted of to a barn where a waiting surgeon amputated the limb with a saw. It was a ghastly experience, but it undoubtedly saved his life. He lived to see his eightieth birthday.

No one can fault the physicians of any era—or the firemen, aviators, sea captains, engineers—for using the knowledge and the tools that were available to them to do their jobs. By this same logic, no one can fault the people of law enforcement for going with the only tool available: incarceration. We have no "good" pills, no "love-your-fellow-man" shots to give to the criminals of our society. All that we can do is separate them from the rest of us and hope they will get the message. And if they don't, then we continue to separate them.

There are some people who argue that prisons do not rehabilitate. I would agree, but at the same time add a heartfelt *So what?* to the proposition. Prisons do not rehabilitate; people rehabilitate. The message must be loud and clear: if you don't want to come back for another stretch, then don't break the law again.

Inherent in this rehabilitation argument is that society does not benefit, because the inmate will come out of prison just as bad—or even worse—than when he entered. What these people overlook is that *society* benefited while the lawbreaker was in prison. If he goes back again, then society will benefit again. Every rapist behind bars means that at least one woman will not be raped today. Every bank robber in jail means that a bank will not be robbed today, and every imprisoned murderer means that an innocent person will live to see another dawn. If we increase the number, it obviously increases the corresponding number of citizens who will escape harm. Prisons are an asset to any society. It really is a simple matter. If the person who would otherwise burglarize your house is already in prison, you come out a winner in the deal.

There are also those who would have us believe that prisons represent a repressive class system. We have all yawned to the old refrain that the rich and powerful do not go to jail, that only the poor are ever convicted. This is absurd. From Nathan Leopold and Richard Loeb to Leona Helmsley, rich people who break the law have gone to jail. When it was announced that F. Lee Bailey was going to defend Patricia Hearst, the wiseacres chanted in a collective chorus she would never spend a day in jail. No one could beat that Hearst–Bailey combination. Yet, she *was* found guilty, and she spent time behind bars. Leopold and Loeb were represented by no less than Clarence Darrow— and Leona Helmsley's attorneys weren't exactly bargain-basement barristers, either.

And what about Watergate? These were "in people" at the White House: Haldeman, Ehrlichman, Colson, *et al.* They also went to prison. Next to the President, there is no one in the country with more legal clout than the Attorney General, but John Mitchell served time as well.

We could even add names such as Walter Wanger, Albert B. Fall, Charles Forbes, Bobby Baker, and William Marcy Tweed, all of whom were wealthy, powerful, or both. There are many names that could be added to such a list, but the point is that the courts do not recognize an elite class that is above the law. As a veteran of four separate tours of jury duty and a member of at least a dozen panels, I have *never* heard a juror suggest that the defendant appeared to be rich, so we had better vote for acquittal. Never, in fact, have I encountered more conscientious and fair individuals than average Americans who are closeted in a jury room, trying to deliver a verdict. They are not dazzled by slick lawyers, and they are not impressed with anyone's income or social standing.

What the *get-to-the-root* people have never quite understood is that crime is an *immediate* problem. If they want to continue hunting for the elusive root, let them proceed, but not at the expense of the feasible and the possible. Until we find a way to prevent people from becoming criminals and harming innocent people, the only sensible plan of action is to put the criminal where he cannot do any additional damage: behind bars.

It was California's one-time governor, Jerry ("Moonbeam") Brown, who said, "Prisons don't rehabilitate, they don't punish, they don't protect, so what in hell do they do?" By merely asking such a question, the speaker reveals the incredible naiveté of the anti-prison crowd. The answer to his question—"What in hell do they do?"—is as simple as it is apparent to the logical mind. Prisons separate the bad guys from the good guys. This is all that they do, and they do it very well. All of the handwringers who go around deploring the lack of rehabilitation during a prison term have lost sight of the basic purpose of that prison, which is to put a wall between the perpetrator and the victim just as a zoo puts a wall between the lion and the zebra. If a prisoner is interested in rehabilitation, we can all wish him success, but if not, another cell will be waiting.

> *Anyone who wants to be a civilized human being has but to stop being a monster.*

In the area of capital punishment, we once again see the handwringers at work, deploring the perceived "cruelty" of it all and fighting to gain lighter sentences for the most vicious predators on the face of this planet. Almost as naive as the Jerry Brown bit about the value of prisons are some of the statements made by that vociferous band of people opposing capital punishment:

1. What will execution accomplish? It certainly won't bring the victim back.
2. We can accomplish the same thing by sentencing murderers to life without parole.
3. Capital punishment is not a deterrent to murder.
4. We should televise executions, because anyone who witnessed one could never support capital punishment again.
5. Capital punishment dehumanizes a society.

Let's look at each of these illogical arguments in turn.

1. *What will execution accomplish?* No, execution will *not* bring the victim back—but who ever said that it would? Imprisonment won't bring the victim back either, nor will a sharp reprimand or requiring the murderer to write "I will not kill people" on the blackboard 100 times. Execution has nothing to do with bringing dead people back to life. It is a punishment for *taking* a human life, by far the worst crime that a human being can ever commit.

2. *Life without parole will accomplish the same thing.*
   There is no such thing as imprisonment without the possibility of parole. As long as a heart
   beats in the chest of a murderer, *someone* will be
   working night and day to put him back on the
   street. A law can be rescinded as easily as it can
   be made, and we have no guarantees whatsoever that the worst of us will not someday again
   be walking among the best of us. Execution set-
   tles the matter permanently.

3. *Capital punishment is not a deterrent to murder.* All
   kinds of statistics have proven that execution is,
   and is not, a deterrent. The two sides can drag
   out the same numbers and debate the issue
   into eternity with very little ever being settled.
   There is, however, another argument that is
   rarely made yet most difficult to counter: anyone who walks the last mile in death row is
   being thoroughly deterred. We can guarantee—absolutely and with certainty—that *this person* will not kill again. People with attractive,
   dark-haired daughters have known since
   January of 1989 that Ted Bundy will never
   again lurk behind the shrubbery.

4. *Televised executions will eliminate support for capital
   punishment.* Televise executions? This is half an
   argument and really proves nothing. If someone would televise the horrible experience of
   an execution simply to prove that it should not
   be allowed, it seems reasonable to precede it
   with a reenactment of the crime as well, as an
   explanation of why the execution is necessary.
   Show the killer as he ties and binds his victims
   in a kneeling position, makes them beg for
   their lives, and then shoots them one by one.
   Show him dragging a teenage girl into his van,

torturing her, raping her repeatedly, and then strangling her and leaving her body in a drainage ditch to die. At this point, we are ready to witness the execution. If we're going to show it, then let's show it all.

5. *Capital punishment dehumanizes society.* Capital punishment does not dehumanize. Premeditated murder dehumanizes. Punishment for a dehumanizing crime is the mark of a civilized society.

The anti-capital punishment crowd—or, more accurately, the anti-*punishment* crowd—has missed the point of execution for as long as any logical person can remember. We are not talking deterrence, and we are not talking rehabilitation. The one and only point to capital punishment is that premeditated murder is a unique crime among all other transgressions. It is not comparable to kidnapping, armed robbery, rape, or insider trading. It is the one crime that must be intolerable to society, and one that in no circumstances will be met with vacillation or indecision. Capital punishment is a social statement that murder is different from all other crimes and will be met with unique punishment. If execution does not deter other murderers, then so be it. It will still make a profound statement about our society: we regard murder as an inexcusable crime, and we will punish accordingly. Every time a door slams for the last time behind a convicted murderer, we reaffirm our status as a civilized society. To tolerate murder is to put ourselves back in the caves, looking for a way to create fire and make axes out of rocks.

When we take a hard-line attitude against crime, we prove that we have matured enough as a civilization to be able to handle the word *No* (this time on a collective basis). It is a social declaration that we will not tolerate crime and will not listen to mealy-mouthed explanations as to why it is acceptable for a specific individual to put his gun to the head of a storekeeper and demand that person's earnings for the day. The *No* argument is that threatening another human being with a gun, knife, rock, or even a pointed stick is never acceptable. Nor is it acceptable to take another person's possessions by force.

> *Nothing is ever gained by tolerating the intolerable.*

I find it difficult to understand the mind of a person who has more compassion for the perpetrator than the victim. The victim of crime is not just the person who suffers a specific injury, but rather anyone who is affected by or in any way pays the price for a crime. Those of us who cannot walk the streets of our cities in safety are victims. People who are forced to put bars over their windows are victims, as are those who must buy alarm systems for their homes, offices, and cars. Victims are those who pay increased insurance premiums to help cover the cost of crime. They pay for the anti-social behavior of others and are victimized every day of the week.

I once had the opportunity to visit a neighborhood in East Los Angeles where the residents lived in total fear of their surroundings. Bars protected the windows of their homes, and many residents had guns (illegally) that were hidden but accessible. They kept a minimum number of lights on at night ("We don't want to call attention to ourselves."), and they chained and double-bolted their doors. No one—I mean *no one*— left their houses at night for any reason. These people were prisoners when the sun went down, and at the same time, thugs became kings. The criminals owned the night, and the police were essentially powerless.

It is a tragic situation when people have no choice but to live like this, and this is the case in many parts of every US city. Decent people live in total fear, and no one seems to care in the least. Activists who spend their time raising money for behaviorally spread diseases and the welfare of people who could do more to help themselves seem oblivious to this obvious, sad reality. If there is a social cause waiting for a white knight, it is definitely the plight of these people who have built their own fortresses and who pray to make it through each night.

> *I would rather see 10 people hungry, or 20 unemployed, than one who is afraid.*

On a recent tour of the Alcatraz penitentiary, much was made of the escape attempts from "the Rock" and of the futility of trying to swim even the relatively short distance (1.5 miles) across San Francisco Bay to the northern shore. Our guides referred to the cold water and strong current, but they said nothing about the people who were there to make the attempt.

Actually, the water is not all that cold. I have spent many happy hours in the pleasant environs of Aquatic Park, watching the sea gulls and the ships passing through the Golden Gate, and it is not at all uncommon to see swimmers in the bay. They won't be wearing wet suits, either. As for the current, it is strong but nothing a good swimmer cannot overcome. In short, it is a difficult—but not impossible—swim, certainly nothing that would require an Olympic-caliber athlete. If you select 100 young men at random from any college campus, military base, or police force, I would say at least 10% could make it from Alcatraz to the shoreline on their first try.

So why were there no successful escapes from Alcatraz? I think that it all goes back to the heart and soul of the criminal. Strong swimmers are dedicated people, just as distance runners, musicians, and honor students are as well. Effort is the cornerstone of excellence; we are talking about something beyond any kind of natural ability or talent. To be a competitive swimmer, one must swim everyday over a period of years.

With absolutely no factual data to back me up, I would say—and without the slightest hesitation—that the young man who spends his adolescence breaking into gum machines, and then advancing to convenience stores and banks, will not be good at anything that requires practice and diligence. There just isn't any correlation between the criminal mind and the pursuit of excellence through practice and goal-oriented perseverance. It seems to be a reasonable conclusion that there probably was not one inmate at Alcatraz in its nearly 30 years of operation who could have gone the distance on a warm day with a boat escort and no one to stop him. The kind of person who would have put forth that much effort into something just wouldn't have wound up at Alcatraz.

Remember, we are not talking about *talent*. There are people in prisons with all kinds of *talent*. I'm talking here about a skill that comes only with diligence and practice. It is the difference between playing the piano by ear and sight reading a classical score, or between doing a slam dunk in the park and playing like Michael Jordan.

It seems reasonable to state that people who go to prison are not disciplined individuals, nor are the criminals on the outside who haven't yet been caught. This is probably why we haven't put our finger on the mercurial "root" of crime, because it is a character flaw that cuts across all strata of society: races, age groups, economic classes, and family backgrounds. Criminals are the flotsam and jetsam of mankind, the derelicts, the undisciplined army of floaters who turn to crime because it takes no training and little skill. We are not talking about people who made "one mistake," but rather the habitual criminal who has opted for a life of lawbreaking. This is the total misfit, incapable of functioning in a society that demands a degree of discipline and responsibility. After all, it is easier to knock over a 7-11 than it is to complete a course in computer repair or learn to be an x-ray technician.

As stated in the quotation that opened this chapter, crime is a *voluntary* thing. The image of Jean Valjean stealing a loaf of bread to feed his family is not the picture of American crime. The criminal is what he is because he makes a conscious decision to flaunt the law and to work in direct opposition to the rules of society. Those who want to sympathize with this kind of behavior have every right to do so, but I heartily wish they would stop blocking the path of those who are trying to solve the problem. As succinctly put in the mini-philosophy of "Lead, Follow, or Get Out of the Way," these people are strongly urged to take the third option.

I have no sympathy whatsoever for the bank robber, the drug dealer, the pimp, the car thief, or the burglar. And to those who would make it easier for these people and give them chance after chance after chance, I ask: What about the rest of us? Don't we count at all? We have only one shot at life, too, and we don't want to live it in fear, hiding behind barred windows with alarm systems cocked and ready. The answer to the whole problem of crime is a simple: support our police departments, build bigger jails, and keep them filled. For those who think this is a "harsh" attitude, be aware that no one is forced to become a criminal. It is a self-made condition. People go to prison because they have done something rotten. Staying out of the lockup is the easiest thing that anyone can do.

The simple truth is that we owe the criminal *nothing*—zero, zip, nada. He brought his own misfortunes on himself, and society is not to blame for the consequences of his chosen lifestyle. Crime is but one more problem that can be solved by the word *No.* The only difference in this case is that we all must say it together.

ADOLESCENCE

---

*No one ever reached maturity through perpetual
concurrence.*

Okay, boys and girls, this chapter is for you.
Frankly, I would rather make my point with
young people, because at this time, there is still
some hope of prying you loose from the positive-
thinking twaddle before it gets an iron grip on
your throat and leads you into a lifetime of bad
decisions and unnecessary trauma. As you step
into young adulthood, you need to recognize
this nonsense for what it is and discard it before
any permanent damage can be done.

I want to wean you away from the emotional
thinking that is so damaging to a useful and productive life. People who make decisions from
their glands rather than their brains are guaranteed to be miserable, and every generation has
the unfortunate experience of learning this all
over again.

I hope to catch one generation on the way up and offer a few tips—dare I say, a *program*—for living a life somewhere on the sunny side of disaster. These few rules for living should lessen considerably your chances of permanent residency in prison or a mental institution. Take heed, my young friends. (As the old cliché goes, someday you will thank me.)

NEVER GO INTO A BATTLE YOU CAN'T WIN

Positive thinkers will never tell you this, but some battles are lost before you ever pick up the gun. There just isn't any point in marching off to war when there is nothing left to win. One example occurs in the workplace, when Dewey and Louie are contending for a promotion. As soon as the choice is made—let's say that Dewey wins— you can be assured that some idiot will advise Louie to march into the superior's office and demand to know why he didn't get the job. This is absolutely the wrong thing to do, because the boss doesn't want to be challenged and will resent the confrontation. The boss will not and cannot admit to a wrong decision, which probably isn't the case anyway, and the challenger will accomplish nothing but to emerge as a complete fool. Once the decision is made, the case is closed. Accept it, and move on to better things.

We can also see the no-win situation at the end of a romance, when one party rudely dumps the other. It is an absolutely futile for the dumpee to plead his or her case. Revenge is a possibility (if one goes in for that sort of thing), but arguing and pleading will accomplish nothing. Dumping is forever.

USE YOUR HEAD WHEN CHOOSING A MATE

Here we move from the general to the specific. My first advice, regardless of your gender, is to look for someone with reasonably good sense; the more intelligent, the better. There can be no hell greater than life with an idiot. Physical endowments wear thin after a period of time—like a weekend—but intelligence has a degree of permanence. Now, for the specifics.

Women

Date the football hero or the "Big Man On Campus," but when you start thinking of marriage, go for the nerd. Believe me, most of the successful men in the world—the movers, the shakers, the people who make things happen—were nerds in high school. Many of them even carried sunglasses and calculators in their pocket protectors. The truth is, the teenage nerd is already far more mature than the campus big shots, the ones who wear the right clothes, use the right language, and move with the assurance of people who have all of the answers. The nerd sees this childish routine but can't work up any enthusiasm, because it registers as immature and trivial. His attentions are directed toward science, music, investments, or maybe the mastery of foreign languages. The one thing that no one ever foresees about the nerd is that at the twentieth class reunion, he will be able to buy and sell everyone in the room.

Men

The most popular girl on campus is usually an airhead. In the adult world, intelligence and popularity are not particularly compatible, but in adolescence, they sit on different sides of a vast chasm. Young men rarely realize that cuteness is a transitory thing, while intelligence and maturity (like diamonds) are forever. Never forget that marriage lasts a lot longer than a short ride on the homecoming float. Married people still have to talk. A good marriage is two people who turn to each other for advice, exchange opinions, and generally help each other become better people. Growing old is a difficult experience under any circumstances, but the problem is compounded tenfold when one marches hand-in-hand with a spouse who never outgrew her jinglebell shoes.

LISTEN TO PEOPLE WHO KNOW MORE THAN YOU

There is probably no bigger falsehood dropped on American youth than this nonsense about "learning from experience." Experience is a very poor teacher. It's the most inefficient way to learn anything. I have never understood the necessity of spending days or weeks learning something that could easily be explained in 10 minutes.

The old experience hogwash is invariably pushed by people who don't like to read and were extremely poor students. The person who says "you just can't learn that in a book" is usually someone who has never *read* a book and hasn't the foggiest idea of what can and cannot be learned from a printed page. When you want to know something that you don't already know, either find an author who is an expert on the subject or talk to someone with some demonstrated skill in that area. Experience represents the hard way of learning anything. It is the armor of the incompetent, the saber of the unlettered, and is always recommended by people who don't know any other way. These are people who would have to jump off of a building to find out that it hurts. The best approach to learning is to listen to the masters. You can always hire people with "experience"; they come cheap.

DON'T BE TALKED INTO TAKING FOOLISH RISKS

There are some risks to almost everything, but use your best judgment and keep the risks to a minimum (certainly less than you can afford to lose). One of the great myths of our time is that one has to take risks to make money. The real moneymakers got where they are by letting *other people* take their risks. They let the suckers put up the money ("You have to take *risks* to make money!"), then cash in when there is a profit to be made. They push this risk principle because they want someone else (you, for example) to put up the money.

The way to wealth is through sound investment. Learn something about economics at an early age (now, for example), and listen to people with a demonstrated ability to acquire wealth. The clown with the big mouth and holes in his shoes is always available to tell you how to make that big score, but all that you have do is look at him. If he knew anything about making money, he would be rich.

> *When the subject is making money, only the rich man is an expert.*

Never—I repeat, *never*—go along with any scheme that mentions "getting in on the ground floor." This simple phrase has caused more financial ruin than anything since Florida swampland. Look for something that is already well off the ground floor, because this is something with a demonstrated ability to rise. I recommend putting your money on the floor below the top, riding it up a notch, then going back for another helping.

As a Californian, I am quite familiar with the lore of the "Gold Rush," which has been romanticized to the point of nausea. The truth is that it was founded entirely on greed, and it featured a pack of idiots charging westward, with no knowledge of gold mining, to make that big score. Very few of them ever made a profit, because there wasn't enough gold to make it worthwhile for a tenth of the throngs who came. The only real money that was made out of the Gold Rush went to the merchants in San Francisco and Sacramento, who were selling these miners their shovels and axes. Hardware is a solid business; gold panning is not. The sad fact is that if another gold rush happened anywhere in the world, the same thing would happen again. The get-rich-quick crowd would do all of the work, while people with the good sense to supply them would make a tidy profit.

Money is made with minimal risk, maximum patience, and a sound knowledge of what you are doing. The beauty of it all is that so few people are willing to believe this, there isn't much competition. So go get it. The world is well stocked with fools who are dedicated to making *you* rich.

REJECT *ALL* FORMS OF POSITIVE THINKING

Positive thinking is a philosophy for people with nothing else going for them. It is a lot of half-mystical nonsense, based on a premise that all kinds of "good things" will happen if you just get the juices flowing and vibrating in a positive way. You don't need this kind of bilgewater to be successful. Success is built on preparation and hard work. Thinking good thoughts has nothing to do with it.

Positive thinking is a raindance philosophy. It tries to tie a successful conclusion to a totally unrelated effort. You can look for results from some form of illusory foot shuffling, or you can step into the real world and *make* things happen. Positive thinking is about a quarter-cut above astrology in having any scientific justification, and it should be treated in about the same way—unless, of course, your cusp is in the Fourth House of the Looney-Toon, in which case you have a good chance of making it all the way down the yellow brick road to the gingerbread house.

LEARN TO EXCEL THROUGH ABILITY

What do Joe Montana, Beverly Sills, Andrew Wyeth, Chris Evert, Van Cliburn, and Jonas Salk have in common, beyond being Americans of the Twentieth Century? All of them are (or were) better than almost anyone else at their chosen callings, and all (start taking notes at this point) subjugated their personalities to their talents. People who truly excel find little need to play the *hey-look-at-me!* game. They don't dye their hair garish colors. They don't wear rings in their noses. They don't tattoo their bodies. They are content with their own excellence, and they let that excellence do the talking.

Outlandish, flamboyant people are invariably those who are starved for any kind of attention, and they lack the intelligence or talent to be noted for what they do. Therefore, they dress like clowns, wear tons of jewelry, and say things that are supposed to be shocking but more often are just loud and undeniably stupid. If you want to be noticed, do it by being better at what you do than anyone else. If this is too difficult, shoot for the top 25. Barring this, you can stand on your head in front of City Hall, but is this really how you want to be noticed? People of genuine accomplishment don't have to resort to this, and neither will you, if you have anything to offer. If you need to be a jerk to get attention, it's far better not to be noticed at all.

ACCEPT WHAT YOU CANNOT DO AS WELL AS WHAT YOU CAN

Few people are more detrimental to human progress than the meddlers. It seems to be a universal human weakness that someone who gains even minimal acclaim in one field feels compelled to spill over into areas where that person is completely incompetent. This is expressed in the Smith Maxim, which I have published several times:

In any human endeavor, the final decision will be made by that person who is the least qualified to make it.

Let's say, for example, that a man makes a fortune in real estate or insurance, then indulges a lifelong wish and buys a professional baseball franchise. It is close to inevitable that within a month he will be questioning trade decisions, and no more than 2 months until he is positioning the outfield. This is a meddler. The actor wants to sing. The singer wants to direct. The director probably wants to tap dance up and down the Capitol Building steps. When this compulsion is accompanied by authority, there is no one to stop the sickness, and we wind up with the inevitable, substandard performance.

Although negativism is considered to be a bad thing, this really isn't true at all. You are not required to go through life saying, "I can, I *can*, I *CAN!*" when in reality you can't. Knowing what you cannot do is really a desirable trait. There is nothing wrong with the word *can't*. An intelligent person is aware of what he cannot do, is never going to be, and leaves this area to people who are good at it. Multitalented people are almost always fairly good at one thing and mediocre in all the rest. I don't think that a real triple-threat halfback ever lived, and I have grave doubts about anyone with a hyphenated occupation. There is, indeed, a cottage industry of book-rewrite people in New York City, whose primary function is to straighten out the messes left by celebrities who think that they can (but can't) write.

Few enough people excel at anything, and once you reach this plateau, you can start by rejoicing and then striving to be even better. Don't push into areas where you have no business being. Accept the fact that somebody is always going to be better than you at something. Carl Sandburg understood this, and so do Lou Holtz and Zubin Mehta. Can we expect anything less from you?

SPEND LESS THAN YOU EARN

This is such a simple law of economics that you can only wonder why it's so often broken. The great scourge of modern existence is debt—overwhelming, suffocating, unrelenting debt. It is a leading cause of divorce, suicide, and mental disorder. The only way to avoid it is to show some self-discipline. If you can't afford it, don't buy it.

ALWAYS LET REASON OVERRULE EMOTION

Never make a major decision based on emotion. This includes marriage, buying a house or a car, or accepting a transfer to another city. Emotions need to be let out and aired occasionally, but the intellect must rule your life.

The answer is always to think ahead. If A leads to B, then B will probably lead to C. Translated, this means that if it didn't work yesterday, it probably won't work today. If the same thing has repeatedly gotten you in trouble, it will get you in trouble again. All acts have consequences, and if these consequences have always been bad, then you just aren't pushing the right buttons. Trouble doesn't end with one serving; as long as you open the door, it just keeps coming back.

AVOID "IN" THINGS AND "IN" PEOPLE

To you, the adolescent, there is probably nothing more important than being *in*: hanging out with the right people, saying all kinds of hip things, and doing all of those things that seem important to a mind just beginning to ripen. Fortunately, most people outgrow this by their early twenties—it's called *growing up*—but a few airheads carry this mentality all the way to senility. It's called the *Beverly Hills Disease*, and it can be easily identified in the form of middle-aged people who actually care about being seen in the right restaurants, shopping in the right stores, and vacationing in places deemed acceptable by the "trendsetters."

These are people to avoid, primarily because they aren't worth knowing. An adult who is concerned with such immature nonsense is undoubtedly someone who has trouble finding his way home at night—an obvious case of mental and emotional arrestment. An adolescent who is trying to become an adult will never make it by associating with people who are stuck at 17 forever.

LIVE DEFENSIVELY

Learn to parry the thrust at an early age. Remember that the world is populated with people who exist by keeping others permanently pinned against the wall. The answer is to stay away from the wall, out of the corners. Have your excuses ready in advance, and become proficient in evasion. Don't be trapped into something that you don't want to do.

Be especially wary of the "hidden-thorn" attack, which is used by people who first find out that you are available and *then* spring the trap. These people begin an invitation with something like, "What are you doing Saturday night?" When this hits, counter immediately with concrete plans. If you say that you have no plans, you've just walked into the shark pool covered with blood. You are already raw meat. You have left yourself wide open. Anyone with a grain of intelligence would begin an invitation or request with an outline of the activity in mind; a born clod will let you expose yourself first and then start pouring the hot oil from his parapet. Invitations offered in this way usually wind up with a painting party in somebody's basement, or a bring-your-own-dinner in a tent, and you have already swallowed the hook. The answer is to be prepared for every eventuality. This is called *defensive living*.

It has often been said that the best defense is a good offense, but I don't think this is always true. In a war, maybe, or in sports, but not in day-to-day living. Here the best defense is a strong, well-planned web of protection that will withstand attack. The ideal situation is to hire a social secretary who can screen everything and keep the gophers from your roses. Most of us can't afford this, however, and are left to our own devices. When this happens, we need imagination, foresight, and determination that we aren't going to be roped into anything. Life is a battle of winners and losers, and the object is to win.

GO TO COLLEGE IF AT ALL POSSIBLE

Most of the people who "couldn't" go to college or who "didn't have the opportunity" are stretching the point more than a little. There have been a few cases in which a young person finished high school, then needed to go to work to support a large number of younger siblings, but such cases are rare. Most people without a college education simply didn't want to do it. It was too much work, and the prospects of going to work and buying a car seemed like a much better road to travel at the time. Later, they could always moan that they didn't have the opportunity, and this would cover a lot of laziness.

The university is often thought of as a place that dispenses knowledge, but this is really a small part of its function. It teaches discipline. It teaches intellectual strength. If nothing else, a college graduate is a reasonably disciplined person. Many high-school graduates complain that the college people get all of the breaks in hiring ("I know as much as that guy knows."), but remember that the interviewer has little to go on beyond a quick conversation and a resume (which could have been written by someone else). With a college degree, the applicant shows the interviewer he had the intestinal fortitude to stay in school at least 4 years, the intelligence to do the required work, and the organizational ability to prioritize all of the requirements and to make everything come out even. Anyone can quit, and many people do. The one who made it all the way has something to enter on the plus side of the ledger.

It is also an interesting and quite valid consideration that college is the first thing a person does in life that isn't mandatory. No one can make this person study, much less pass the courses, and anyone who is bent on flunking out will fail. The one who elects to remain and finish a job that was started shows a notable bit of character at an early age. It isn't an infallible test, but it is right more often than wrong. We know for a fact that a quitter has shown us nothing at all.

DON'T LISTEN TO COUNSELORS WITH NO ACADEMIC CREDENTIALS

There is no information easier to obtain than the list of accredited colleges and universities. Libraries and bookstores have this information, and the nominally priced *Information Please Almanac* carries a complete listing of all such institutions. Thus, the practitioner with a "Doctorate" in Astro-Baloney from Storefront Academy can be readily exposed—and should be.

As far as astrology and palmistry are concerned, I wouldn't let one of these people counsel my cat. These "professionals" are about a half-step removed from the fortune teller's tent—and usually about as well educated. Many of them work with the title "Doctor"—there are unfortunately no laws against this practice—but their degrees are about as legitimate as stock in the Brooklyn Bridge. They have no business counseling or advising anyone.

If you need help with a problem, go to someone who has taken the trouble to earn his stripes, to establish a recognized position in a legitimate academic discipline. In short, go to someone who knows what he's talking about. You won't regret it.

DO NOT EVEN *CONSIDER* A NONMARITAL LIVING ARRANGEMENT

The argument always made for such a living arrangement is that if it doesn't work out, then both parties can simply walk away and no one is hurt. This never happens, however, because the argument is based on the supposition that both parties will come to the realization at the same time. (All together now, "Hey, it isn't working out. Let's split!") Life just isn't this tidy. The inevitable ending is that one person walks, and the other is dumped. It's called *reality*.

Actually, a shack-up (well, that's what it is) represents the worst of both worlds, of single life and marriage. It lacks the respectability and commitment of a marriage, yet there isn't the freedom of a single life, either. People who live together do not date other people—at least not openly—and they are still required to call home when they aren't going to make it for dinner. I just cannot imagine why any single person would willingly opt for this no-win situation.

As you grow older, you will probably have someone suggest such an arrangement. Don't do it. Go for the fulfillment of a traditional marriage, or stay single and swing. Don't settle for the worst of each.

ACCEPT THE WORD *NO* AS THE BEST FRIEND YOU'LL EVER HAVE

This is the most important of all rules; therefore, I have saved it for the last. Put in its simplest form, when you can say *No*, then you will be in control of your own life.

You have to take control of your life, and you aren't too young to start. You can listen to the myths, the half-truths, and the general nonsense of the sunshine philosophers, or you can put your brain into gear and start moving forward on the solid impetus of your intellect. Emotional thinking will lead you to the poor house, a mental institution, or prison. Reject it. Go with reason and logic. There is nothing better I can tell you.

8

THE CORPORATE MENTALITY

---

*To grant authority to a jackass is to turn
dormant stupidity into dynamic incompetence.*

As a long-time player in corporate America, I
know the strong tie between boardroom thought
processes and positive thinking, the gibberish
that has been so much a part of our lives for the
past 50 years. I can state without the slightest
hesitation that my upward mobility ended with
the publication of *How To Cure Yourself Of Positive
Thinking.*

That book questioned the most hallowed
tenet of the corporate mentality, and the philosophy I advanced was taken as something that
struck at the vitals of the hierarchy (like telling
Mrs. Vanderbilt that her daughter was going to
marry a Baptist). I am still at a loss to understand why any profit-making enterprise would
object to a philosophy that stressed rational
thought, but I found I had inadvertently taken a
pot shot at a sacred cow.

To the uninitiated, it seems odd that Big Business would cling so tightly to a principle of such questionable credibility. After all, corporate mentality is supposed to be a hard-headed, dollars-and-cents kind of thing, one that doesn't receive half-baked ideas with much enthusiasm. Yet, it has swallowed the hook on positive thinking, and it has shown no signs of letting go.

I think the explanation for this otherwise unexplainable phenomenon rests in a chance occurrence of bull's-eye timing. The positive-thinking absurdity was unloaded on the American public during the 1950s, about the same time that Big Business was being influenced by Harvard, Stanford, and the rest of the tweed-suit crowd to establish "enlightened" management. Under the terms of this new credo, the boss was supposed to "get closer" to the employees, to "care." (Does anyone remember "togetherness?") Suggestion boxes began appearing on the walls of every factory, and grievance committees were created to hear the complaints of the rank and file. No one was very serious about playing this game, but they all took a place at the table.

The time was fast approaching when a boss could no longer say, "Do it because I said to do it!" The spirit remained, though. Management was groping for a less-offensive way of saying the same thing. Then, suddenly, out of nowhere, came *positive thinking*, like the White Knight riding out of the royal forest. Now the boss could say, "I want a good, positive attitude," which translated into the same message but went down a lot better, like medicine hidden in syrup.

In business parlance, a *positive attitude* means that people are supposed to cooperate and not object to anything. It is actually one of the most manipulative phrases ever introduced into the business world, and it is more often used to club heads than to wring excellence from the human soul. To object is to be *negative*, and this is the all-purpose no-no of the Twentieth Century.

Positive thinking gave business exactly what it wanted, and at a time when it was desperately needed. It provided the opportunity to go on governing with a sledgehammer and yet appear to be "enlightened" at the same time. From this came the idea of the *team player*, which is a wonderful euphemism for someone who looks the other way when the Cossacks plunder the village.

When I entered corporate America directly out of college, I was given some invaluable advice by an older employee, and I found it difficult (but not impossible) to accept it. As it was spelled out to me then, the company did not want to see boat rockers, and such people were immediately marked with an indelible stamp and considered unpromotable. The basic idea was to swallow one's integrity during business hours and to be a part of the "team"—a term, incidentally, that I still find rather nauseating to this day.

I said this was difficult but not impossible to accept, because I soon learned it was folly to stand up for a principle that no one wanted anyway. It was a lot like saving a woman from an attacker, then seeing her walk off with him, hand in hand, while you lay bleeding on the sidewalk. There is a time for courage and a time to mind one's own business.

I participated in programs that cost twice as much as they should have because of mismanagement, and I slavishly followed the orders of some of the most incompetent and mentally deficient human beings I have ever encountered. I saw and tolerated waste and bungling that staggered the imagination. I saw boat rockers hung out to dry, with none of their peers having a kind word to say about them. They were dead in the water and quite alone, with the only thoughts ever expressed being that they should have "known better." I learned to keep my mouth shut and to view incompetence and inefficiency as necessary parts of living, much like toothaches and houseflies. For my team-player services, I was rewarded with regular salary increases and promotions commensurate with my tenure.

It all came to an end, however, with the publication of my first book, which never mentioned the company or was in any way an attack on its management. It did, however, question the holy icon of positive thinking, and for this, I was given the "degradation shuffle," which is management's way of encouraging an employee in disfavor to leave voluntarily (easier on everyone, you know) and thus save the company a lot of trouble. I was shunted off to meaningless assignments in remote buildings, made to work for people who once worked for me, and generally humiliated on a daily basis. The weekly staff meeting is a good example of the way that it was handled. I had attended regular Friday-morning meetings for about 5 years, when suddenly the time and place of the meeting changed every week and I was never informed. The boss always "forgot" but would surely inform me the next time, which he never did. (Write a book about positive thinking, will you?)

Fortunately, I started selling my work about that time, so I could ride out the situation with a light at the end of the tunnel. There were, however, so many others dancing the degradation shuffle that it left me with a permanent bad taste in my mouth. One wonders how the orchestrators can justify their actions—except to say that they are "team players."

One friend of mine fell into disfavor and had his desk (literally) turned to face the wall. Then he was given no work to do. At first, this seems to be an ideal situation, to go in and goof off all day and be paid for it. In reality, there is nothing even remotely pleasant about it. There was a rule about reading at one's desk, or working crossword puzzles, so this eliminated any kind of personal entertainment. He had no assignments in other parts of the plant, so there was no excuse to leave the desk, except to go to the men's room (and this time was carefully monitored). Excessive time away from the work station was a violation of company rules and grounds for dismissal, as were excessive absenteeism and nonbusiness phone calls. So, this man had the choice of staring at the wall or quitting, which he did after about 3 weeks of the degradation shuffle.

The concept of the "team" is ostensibly harmless enough. After all, what objection could anyone have to the idea of everyone pulling together toward a common goal? The answer, simply, is that it works on the playing field (where it belongs) but has no place in business or the professional world, where grown people work, think, and create. It is inappropriate, because it demands unquestioned support for all projects, especially the bad ones.

There must have been someone at Ford who thought the Edsel was a bad idea, that a market slot just did not exist for it. I am sure someone at Lockheed fought the L1011 fiasco, and there were undoubtedly people at JC Penney and Sears who wanted to stay with the product line that had put them in the hearts and minds of the American consumer. All of these companies got into trouble with bad ideas, and these bad ideas were all endorsed by team players who weren't about to question anything.

I am sure there were team players who told Adolf Hitler that invading the Soviet Union was a good idea, that there were positive thinkers who supported Pickett's Charge and the Maginot Line. There is no idea so bad that it can't get support from *someone*, and if the upper levels back it, then you can go to the bank with a universal blessing.

There can be no objection to cooperating in the completion of a project, but it should be accepted as a general rule and not an edict from Heaven. If there is a flaw in the plan, it should be uncovered, and who better to point it out than the people who will be carrying the spears into battle?

A good example of management marching off in the wrong direction occurs with the inevitable "economy wave," which rocks through most organizations on a regular basis. No one can object to the idea of cutting costs, but the economy wave is always implemented from the top down. Management makes arbitrary personnel cuts—usually the best people—and merges departments that should never be merged. Why don't they work from the bottom up? Almost every worker knows how his function could be done more efficiently, but no one ever asks them. Time and again I have seen muscle stripped from the bone while the fat remained, but objections were futile. (I wasn't going to be keelhauled with the agitators.) I could have saved my company a fortune without costing a single job by cutting unnecessary overtime, streamlining the operation, and putting competent people (real managers) in charge. No one asked, however, and I didn't volunteer my thoughts, spending nearly 20 years as a valuable and trusted team player. I always adopted a positive attitude, even though I silently watched untold dollars being flushed down the toilet.

Cost cutting is always done on safe levels—a lot like driving a Jaguar in the slow lane. An example of this occurred with the Great Paper Clip Caper, which I saw firsthand over a decade ago. One of the hourly employees in our company noticed a paper clip box on his desk, and he read on the label that there were supposed to be 100 clips inside. It was a new box. He knew that none of the clips had been removed. When he counted them, however, he found only 97 clips. He went to the supply cabinet then, brought out other new boxes, and counted them all. There were fewer than 100 in each one. Following this, he spent the next few lunch hours counting every paper clip box in sight, and he found that we were being shorted regularly by a few clips. He made his findings known to his superiors, who passed the report to the top echelons. This discovery was well received, because it was *safe*. It didn't tread on anyone's toes or highlight the incompetence of anyone's brother-in-law. The young man was commended, and an article about him appeared in the company paper, along with the information that the paper clip supplier had been contacted and planned to make full restitution for the missing clips, along with assurances that all boxes henceforth would contain 100 clips. In its import as a news item, it was treated like nothing less than the D-Day Landing.

The article appeared on a day when I was holding 17 people—on overtime pay, no less—waiting for one indecisive man to release the work that should have come to us that morning. The company could have recovered the price of *every paper clip in its entire history* simply by replacing this klutz with someone who could make a decision. We burned money as though it were stacks of autumn leaves, all the while marching to glory with the Great Paper Clip Victory.

This one individual, incidentally, brought me considerable wealth in a 5-year feeding frenzy of unnecessary overtime. I put a new roof on my house, enlarged my patio, and installed an air-conditioning system, all because of one disorganized person who gummed up the works with an amazing predictability. The company would not allow any criticism of this man, either. (It was a "sensitive issue.") So, we all fattened up accordingly and kept the home contractors in business, except for the apartment dwellers who were content with visiting foreign shores. Still, management was delighted to be compensated for at least 100 paper clips and to realize that conscientious employees were alert to available cost savings.

It seems rather cynical at this late date to recount these parallel incidents, but this sort of thing is occurring over and over again in business and in government. Industry in particular hurts itself immeasurably when it refuses to look at the real problems and applauds the safe solutions as though they were the salvation of mankind.

The real culprit is positive thinking, because it promotes mindless game playing and discourages honest and meaningful contributions. No one in private industry is as despised as the boat rocker, and once this stamp is applied to your forehead, it never rubs off. Intelligent, capable people are forever bypassed for promotions, and incompetent people rise to authority solely by not offending anyone. They are—of course—team players. The simple truth is that anyone with a grain of integrity has offended *someone*, and I am not interested in knowing anyone who hasn't.

Back in my positive-thinking, team-player days, I once worked for a man who had a pronounced prejudice against people with college degrees. He didn't have one himself, and he didn't like anyone who did. He chose a man with 1 year of community college as his managerial assistant, and most of his supervisors (whom he inherited) were people with bachelor's degrees. I was one of them. I had a person with an MA and another with a PhD working for me. It was absolutely ludicrous, but no one in top management objected, nor was it ever questioned. Eventually, the college-educated supervisors were replaced with high-school dropouts, and this seemed to make everyone happy. There wasn't a negative thought expressed.

No one in management wants to be second-guessed by subordinates. By the same token, however, no one is infallible. If a subordinate has something to contribute, the world isn't going to end if someone listens. Change does not always have to originate at the top.

The biggest problem facing American industry today stems directly from the misapplication of positive thinking. As originally intended, it is a harmless philosophy, one that won't really help anyone but hasn't been known to cause headaches, skin irritations, or shortness of breath. When twisted, however, and used as a weapon, it can be deadly. Industry uses it as a device to implement bad decisions. Anyone who questions an unworkable idea is branded as *negative*, and this is the kiss of death, not only in business but in the general framework of society. Positive people (team players) are those who get behind a program of abysmal stupidity, then ride it all the way to financial ruin.

American industry has seen one product line after another go to foreign manufacturers, not because they did it better but because they had a better grasp of the market than the American suppliers. Nor can any of it be blamed on bad times. The market is still there; it is just bending in another direction. The automobile is a classic example. Detroit was still building its oversized, overchromed jukeboxes in the 1970s when the Japanese took the market away by offering a product people wanted. Again, we see bad decisions, horrendous decisions, all backed by the full authority to go charging down the wrong road with thousands of positive-thinking sycophants applauding wildly in the background.

I believe that the greatest contribution anyone can ever make in our society is to kill a bad idea. When this power is curtailed, everyone loses, because stupidity and inefficiency are given the freedom to grow and to flourish. There is a general belief that if nothing else, dictatorship is more efficient than democracy because "things get done." Most people agree that they wouldn't want to live in a dictatorship, but they also grudgingly admit that it *is* more efficient. Whatever the strong man wants is done and with minimal interference.

This is a surface truth, however. The real world doesn't work this way. Supreme, unquestioned power enables a leader to implement bad as well as good decisions. Whether the decision is to invade a neighboring country or bring out a product that won't sell, unbridled power gives a leader full authority to be wrong. Dictatorships are built on the false assumption that the leader will consistently be right, but this has yet to be the case. Dictators are destroyed because they are free to make the colossal blunders that bring about their own ruination. (Remember the Soviet Union, anyone?)

Another danger of absolute power is the need for total, unquestioning loyalty in one's subordinates. Rather than selecting a qualified staff on the basis of ability, the strong man surrounds himself with toadies, people who will do his every bidding. Therefore, the implementation of his ideas (even the good ones) will be second rate. If I were put into a position of political power, I would much rather have a Rush Limbaugh or a Barry Goldwater questioning my every move than a Hermann Goering telling me I am a genius.

Democracy is essentially inefficient, but it contains a built-in mechanism to destroy bad ideas. Even the good ones have a devil of a time making it through to fruition, but the sacrifice is worth the gain. Look at it as a tradeoff. It is far better to kill a bad idea than to implement a good one, so in the long run, we all benefit in some way from the strangulation of red tape—unbelievable as that might sound.

All of this political talk applies directly to the business world. A leader who is empowered to do what he wants, without opposition, runs the danger of making catastrophic mistakes. I realize that business is not a democracy, nor should it be, but there must be opposition. When the "good, positive attitude" prevails, opposition is impossible. The leader who won't allow negativism won't allow opposition either, and this is the road to destruction.

SELFISHNESS HAS ITS POINTS

You owe nothing to anyone who owes nothing to you.

I knew Leslie several years ago when we worked together in Los Angeles. She was divorced and the mother of two teenage daughters. Leslie married a man who also worked with us, and it was a very good match. Everyone was quite happy about the whole thing. It was the termination of her first marriage, however, that I think provides a lesson for anyone who is willing to listen.

Her first husband—the father of her children—was a drunk. Leslie had put up with his drinking for years. She went through his brief periods on the wagon, his promises never to drink again, and the great, gut-wrenching disappointments when he would come home late and pass out on the bed.

On the last of these occasions, he lost his wife and his two children, all while he was unconscious: a terrible price for that last drink. Leslie experienced a revelation, the kind that occurs so rarely in one's lifetime. As she tells it, there was no emotion involved. During a time of maximum stress, she made a cold, rational decision, because that decision had to be made. She looked at this disgusting lump lying across the bed and knew that her marriage was over. Above all, she stopped caring if he went on drinking or not. His problem was no longer her problem. Leslie got her children out of bed, packed their bags, and moved that night. In her mind, she saw two choices. One was to continue with a dead-end life, crying herself to sleep every night and hoping for something that was never going to happen. The other was to end it and begin all over again. It was that simple. And at that precise moment, she wrote him off, separated herself from a problem that was no longer hers, and turned in a direction that would provide some happiness for both herself and her daughters.

The husband made some impassioned phone calls over the next few weeks, promising all kinds of personal rebirth if she would only take him back. Leslie refused. The decision had been made, and to her credit, it was irrevocable. She wrote him off like a bad debt.

I have said repeatedly in these pages that personal problems must be solved intellectually, not emotionally, and this is exactly what Leslie did. Indeed, it was what she had to do. In a moment of rare insight, she recognized her husband as a source of unending disruption and misery, then she cut the man out of her life. The most important factor in her new attitude was that she stopped caring. From that moment on, the man was free to drink himself to death without scolding, nagging, or pleading from any quarter. He became a "nonperson" to her.

This, I firmly believe, is the way that many of our problems need to be met and solved. If a person causes nothing but misery to others, the only solution is the write-off. You can become part of someone else's perpetual problem and suffer from things that you did not cause, or you can distance yourself from the whole mess and start to live your own life, responsible for your own mistakes and only your own.

The resistance to this solution is always emotional. ("I just can't turn my back. After all, this is my [mother, father, sister, brother, son, daughter, old friend, second cousin, take your pick].") This is the emotional approach, and it has yet to solve anything. The perennial problem case is going to bring *you* into the middle of the self-made bag of misery, and you will stay there as long as emotion rules your life.

We are taught as children that we must never be selfish, which is fine if we're talking about tinker toys or electric trains. When it comes to living, however, we sometimes have to be selfish to survive (and certainly to be happy).

I spoke with a lady shortly after the publication of *How To Cure Yourself Of Positive Thinking*, and she told me that her 28-year-old daughter had brought her nothing but grief for the previous 12 years. The girl had been a drug user and was expelled from high school. She had been arrested several times, had lived with men who physically abused her, had shoplifted, and generally had made one stupid and destructive decision after another. The mother was involved because the daughter periodically came home for a brief rest and regrouping before the next series of misadventures. The mother repeated the old hand-wringing refrain of "Where did I go wrong?" which solved nothing. (Whining never does.)

My advice to her—as it is to *all* people in her shoes—was to drive the snakes from the garden. When one person brings nothing but misery into the life of another, then that person simply has to go. In effect, it is an act of divorce. The troublemaker becomes a non-person. Remember that we are *not* talking about the traditional helping hand. Most of us are quite willing to help a friend with unforeseen difficulties. We are dealing here with the *chronic* problem case, someone who is, always has been, and always will be a problem to other people. You don't need this person in your life. No one does. And you have to muster the strength to do something about it.

It must also be remembered that no game can be played by two sets of rules. The person who is causing the problems is being utterly selfish, caring nothing about the feelings or welfare of the people who are being dragged into the mess. It would seem only reasonable to think that the other players in the game should be allowed to be selfish as well. You have the right to ask a favor of me, and I have the right to refuse. These rules should make sense to everyone involved.

Sometimes, the rationale for the offending person's actions is "sickness," which is the all-purpose excuse for any kind of anti-social behavior. We are supposed to accept the assertion that nasty, ill-mannered, rude, and generally offensive people are really "sick," and that we are obliged to put up with them because they can't help themselves. Rubbish! When these people have enough doors slammed in their faces, they might just find a "cure."

The selfishness I advocate is reactive in nature. I am not saying that you should cut the biggest piece of pie for yourself, or refuse to accept reasonable family and social obligations. Constructive selfishness is a wall that protects a person from unwanted incursions. Chronic, self-made, and never-ending problems belong to the creator of those problems, and they do not need to be shared. You are under no obligation to help a person who makes no effort to help himself. If you learn nothing else in your journey through life, learn this. I have used the word *reactive*; you do not initiate the selfishness but employ it only as a reaction to those who make unreasonable demands on you. It is a defensive weapon, and it should be used in only this way. When it is used, however, go with both barrels.

Getting back to the matter of "sickness," we should see this for what it is. In a very general sense, we might agree that anyone who commits a crime, or any flagrant anti-social act, might be a bit "sick," but this is an abstract concept. Anyone who could commit an act of rape or kidnap and terrorize a child must be something of a mental case, but we should not equate this someone who is unable to function because of a physical malady that he did not invite. *That* is sickness.

Frankly, this sickness routine makes me a little— well, *sick*. People who drink too much like to think they have a disease, which gets them around the problem by saying they are not responsible. (To quote the old Flip Wilson line, "The Devil made me do it.") People who steal from stores, run up huge debts on their credit cards, neglect their families, refuse to work, shoot illegal drugs into their veins, even those who eat too much are said to be suffering from diseases and not to be censured for their actions. I wouldn't be at all surprised to read about the newly discovered "Bonnie-and-Clyde Disease," which forces otherwise decent people to rob banks. (I don't even want to think about the "Jeffrey Dahmer Disease.")

The flip side of the coin is that these people consistently lean on the solid citizens who aren't "allowed" to have diseases and therefore must pick up the tab for the rest of society. I have never been allowed to have one of these so-called diseases. If I should take something from a store, I would be a thief, which would be quite true, and I would go to jail. Society allows me to have the flu about once every third year, and this is the extent of it. ("No more diseases for you, Smith! We need you for *leaning!*")

The best definition I have yet heard for a disease is "a morbid condition of a human organ," which means that part of the anatomy has been visited by an incursive microorganism or pathogenic agent that will cause death if not arrested. This, in the proverbial nutshell, is a *disease.* Putting a bottle to one's mouth and drinking the liver into abject surrender is not a disease. A weakness, most assuredly, and an addiction, but not a disease. Spending more than one earns is not a disease. Neither is a sex drive that injures other people. These things are a sign of human weakness and personal irresponsibility—sometimes even depravity—and no one so engaged is in any way a "victim." When you can solve your problem by stopping whatever it is that you are doing, you do not have a disease.

To instill an attitude of constructive selfishness, we have to rid ourselves of the "obligation" burden. People who live with perpetual obligation to others are really *slaves.* They don't control the situation, and they spend their whole lives reacting to the demanding and unreasonable behavior of someone else.

It is the receivers who perpetuate the obligation game and keep the you-owe-me business alive. And why shouldn't they as long as it works? No one ever seems to turn the situation around and ask what these people owe anyone else. The entire thing has been reduced to a single formula by my friend, the aforementioned Sage of Bakersfield, who advances the *Two-Mess Rule* as a guide for both the leaners and the leaned-on. Under this arrangement, one person will bail another person out of a mess twice in a lifetime.

That's all. Two times and you're through. No more credit.

The Sage told me that he once let an ever-needy cousin be evicted from his home, because he (the Sage) had once come out in the middle of the night and towed this man's car from a ditch. On another occasion, he put up the bail money to get him out of jail. The man had used his two chances, and that was it as far as the Sage was concerned. The cousin never spoke to him again, of course, but the Sage opined that losing this person's friendship was like losing a canker sore (and he had no regrets).

Actually, the Two-Mess Rule isn't a bad one at all. There is nothing magic about the number, however, and it could just as well be one or three. The important thing is that there should be a limit placed on the demands of the Problem Perennial. There must be a time when the saturation point is reached and someone says *enough*. After you have done it once, it is such a good feeling that you will want to do it again.

When employed sensibly and responsibly, selfishness can be a desirable thing indeed. I think there is a definite tie-in here with the writings of the great German philosopher Immanuel Kant. It was Kant who formulated the Categorical Imperative:

Act as if the maxim of your action were to become through your will a general natural law.

This is an ethical principle that is applicable to our daily conduct, and it most certainly can be applied to everything that has been discussed in this chapter. It is actually a spin-off from the Golden Rule, and various people have expressed it in different ways, including the contemporary "What goes around comes around" (and that grand old favorite of the US Navy, "Shape up, or ship out!"). Kant is saying that we should act at all times as though we would want our actions to become an acknowledged universal law. In the case of the leach-and-loser write-off, do we want this to become general practice in our day-to-day living? I suggest that we do. It is only fitting that the personal write-off become the natural way of things. If this actually did come to pass, then after repeated offenses:

- The drunk and the drug abuser would face the consequences of their actions alone. No one would plead with them to get help or to straighten themselves out.
- Bad check artists would go to jail. No one would show up to cover the loss.
- People who spend the rent money at the track would be evicted.
- Anyone running from police or bill collectors would be given no place to hide.
- The deadbeat who needs immediate cash to get out of a mess would be thrown right back into that mess.
- Philandering spouses would not get back inside the door.
- The habitual liar would be exposed and discredited.

Would we be any worse off today if any of this happened? I think not. We need these people like we need ringworm, and I see no point in prolonging a situation that isn't going to end until the exploited party ends it. The person who lives off the body heat of productive society certainly isn't going to call a halt to any of it.

> *An invader either stays or is driven out; he never leaves voluntarily.*

The happiest people in the world are those who understand selfishness, and who realize that it has a worthwhile place in human existence. These people put limits on their charity, and they know exactly how far it will bend before the bending even starts. They truly control their own lives, and without control, there can be no happiness.

When we think of selfishness, let us see it in terms of self-interest rather than self-indulgence. It is not a matter of keeping all of the toys, but rather of setting limits so that a certain part of one's existence is not open to exploitation. Think of it as a sort of Monroe Doctrine for the soul. This person says to the world, "Enjoy me for what I am, not for what I can do for you."

It seems like a reasonable thing to ask.

FACING LIFE WITH A GOOD NEGATIVE ATTITUDE

Don't waste time feeling sorry for yourself. Spend it constructively, getting even with the one who stuck it to you.

Now that we have realized the need for enlightened negativism in our lives, it is time to get to the practicality of the matter. So, let's begin to apply it.

The first step is to develop a familiarity, a comfortable working arrangement, with the word *No.* Hopefully, this word will now form the cornerstone of your thought processes. Stand in front of the mirror and watch yourself as you repeat it softly, with vigor, rapidly, slowly and with feeling, then topping it off with the drill-sergeant crescendo. Let it roll as a thundering paean to the heavens. You might work it into musical form, or possibly even give a cheer: "Gimme a *N!* Gimme an *O!* What's it spell?! *Nooooooooo!*"

The word must come out flowingly or, as Hamlet said, "trippingly on the tongue." It must come from the depths of your soul and emerge as easily and naturally as a cough or a sneeze. It must be said without hesitation and without qualification—which means with no excuses. Above all, it must be said with finality, with the assurance that it will never be retracted, and this is probably the hardest part of all. Once spoken, it must be cast in concrete, eternal.

Many people who have trouble saying *No* find themselves buying things they really don't want because an aggressive salesperson has worn them down. In some cases, the item is actually bought out of fear. They have been cowed and intimidated by the salesperson. This is an excellent arena to practice in, because sales resistance is often the key to developing a mastery of this magic word. You are now learning at the knee of the master, because there is little doubt that I have more sales resistance than anyone now breathing on this planet. The more a salesperson insists that I buy a product or service, the greater my resolve not to. Cold, steely resolve is a strong defense, and a flash of anger is always a fitting coup de grâce to end this battle.

Salespeople have several techniques to burrow in at your first sign of weakness. One of these is to remind the pigeon—you—of personal responsibilities. Those selling insurance or home security systems regularly bring this one into play. ("If you don't buy what I'm selling, you're not meeting your responsibilities to your family.")

Do *not* fall for this one. When they use this approach, and assuming that you might want to go beyond a well-spoken and definitive *No*, you can leap forward in obvious indignation and be shocked that anyone would have the *audacity* to question your adequacy as a provider and protector, stopping just short of screaming, "Go, you cad, and never darken my doorway again!" This is one of the few instances in which I advocate taking the offensive. I am a defensive fighter at heart, but once in awhile this can be fun.

Another technique often used is that based on *your* ability to help *him*. Be ready for this one, because many door-to-door salespeople trot out this old chestnut. They are usually gathering points to be applied toward some noble endeavor, and you are somehow under an obligation to help them. As you set up your defenses, remember that the person who is trying to sell you something should be primarily interested in you and your needs, your welfare, your appearance, your health, your financial situation, and so on. You owe nothing to anyone who arrives on your porch unannounced and uninvited and then tries to sell you something. If it is something that you want and at a price you are willing to pay, then go ahead and buy it. Otherwise, the answer must be *No*.

Another commonly used approach is the rather crude battle of wills. Once an aggressive salesperson spots a chink in your armor, he will muster all forces and go on the attack. In this case, you have to be stronger, which is why I advocate practice in front of a mirror.

I offer here the *Resistance Formula*, which can be stated simply as $P = R + 1$. In other words, pressure (P) will always be met by an equal amount of resistance (R) plus one additional unit of force. As the pressure increases, so does the resistance, so we could easily write the equation as $P^3 = R^3 + 1$, always one unit ahead. It is not unlike the mechanical rabbit at the dog track, which is always a bit faster than the fastest dog. In this way you will never—I repeat *never*—buy anything that you don't want again.

I actually like to deal with aggressive salespeople from time to time, just to keep the reflexes honed and to stay in good negative trim. There is not the slightest chance I am going to buy anything I don't want, but I still like to practice my negative skills. I enjoy seeing the expression on the aggressor's face when he realizes he has run into a rock. I have always contended that defense is far more important than offense, and here we see the principle in practice for anyone to see.

It distresses me when I hear someone explain that he "bought it to get rid of the salesman." First, this isn't quite true. It also isn't even a clever ploy, because the salesman clearly won and the buyer lost. More important is the fact that it is such a mealy-mouthed, cringing excuse that it demeans anyone who speaks these words. One wonders about the character of anyone who buys something simply to be spared the sales pitch. How will this person handle any other situation in life? Probably by caving in. Never buy anything just to get rid of the salesman. You tell him *No* and then get rid of him.

I advocate practicing sales resistance because it is such wonderful training once you determine to improve your negative skills. It is good to start with door-to-door salespeople, because you operate from your own turf and therefore have a security blanket for support. When your skills and resolve are functioning adequately, you can go into their lair—an insurance office, for example—and practice holding out. The final test, and the one that only real pros dare to tackle, is the big automobile dealership. By *big*, I mean one that advertises a lot, especially on television, and employs a small army of cannibals who live by jumping on the flesh and not letting go until somebody signs some papers. I have been through this routine on numerous occasions in Los Angeles, where no quarter is given, and I can see how it might be a frightening experience for anyone who has trouble saying *No* on a far less-intensive level.

As I have said, this is the supreme test, and it probably isn't necessary for anyone who only wants to obtain the adequate negative skills for daily living. It is, however, something to shoot for, like getting an advanced degree at a university, and certainly can do a lot to build your confidence. Anyone who can make it through the minefield of a major car dealership is well prepared for any eventuality. The brother-in-law with the hand out is like a parlor game for anyone who has swum with the sharks.

The little word *No* is easily the most powerful word in the English language. It is the greatest force for good in the entire lexicon, and I can think of no better morale builder. People who consistently cave in under pressure never feel good about themselves. Giving "another chance" to someone who doesn't deserve it is guaranteed to make anyone feel completely inadequate, and more like a worm than a person. Standing up and saying *No*, however, is an experience not unlike being reborn.

Several years ago, a very misunderstood First Lady was ridiculed without mercy for her *Just-Say-No* solution to the drug problem. If anyone stopped to consider the statement seriously, however, they would realize that Nancy Reagan was absolutely right. In real life, the user has the choice of saying *No* or eventually giving his life for that last fix. This is the way that problems are solved.

The alcoholic can join a support group, undergo psychoanalysis, try hypnosis, try religion, or even quit cold turkey on his own. In the final analysis, however, it all comes down to the same unavoidable conclusion. The alcoholic must quit drinking. The alcoholic must say *No*. This is not an oversimplification. It is an eternal and undeniable truth. The various treatments and approaches to this problem are merely methods of getting to the same place. The solution to alcoholism or drug addiction is to *quit*. Everything else is just another way of getting there.

All of the people mentioned in this book had to say *No* to someone or something. Nora had to back off and let Bill handle Daphne. Art and Marilyn had to stand up to their relatives in Wisconsin. Leslie had to face a situation that wasn't going to correct itself and leave her husband. These people all said *No*—perhaps a bit late in some cases, but they all said it—and they were immeasurably better off for doing it.

Somewhere along the line, we have been taught that it is bad to be negative. If you believe this, ask yourself where being *positive* has ever gotten you. To be positive is to allow people to walk all over you, and there is absolutely no justification for this. There is hardly any human problem that cannot be resolved by saying *No*.

Let me tell you about Myrna. I would like to say she was a friend, but I never met the lady. She was actually a friend of my grandparents, something of a legend in our family, and she passed away when I was very young. Myrna was the only girl in a family of five children, and she was the next to youngest. The family lived on a farm in upstate New York, somewhere in the vicinity of Syracuse. The mother died when Myrna was 13, and it was "decided" that she would take over all duties as homemaker, which was generally accepted as being "woman's work." She would do all of the cooking, cleaning, ironing, and laundry, all with no help from her father or brothers. She somehow made it through high school and then decided she was going to college. Of course, this idea was met with total resistance by all five males, who couldn't fry an egg much less wash a shirt, and she was told in no uncertain terms that she was not going to leave home and go traipsing off to college. Her job was to stay home and look after her father and brothers. They needed a drudge, and Myrna was elected. In fact, it was a landslide victory.

What they didn't know was that Myrna, an excellent student, had applied for a college scholarship already and been granted a completely free ride through a major university. She left home despite the objections, and she went on not only to earn a bachelor's degree but stayed for a master's degree as well. Eventually, she moved to the West Coast, started her own business, and died a half-century later as a wealthy and respected lady. Her brothers, it can be assumed, learned somewhere along the line to put a peanut-butter sandwich together and survived.

I heard this story of Myrna and her accomplishments many times when I was growing up, but it was only a few years ago when I learned the story of her departure. It seems that in the week before she left for the university, her father and brothers quit speaking to her. Instead of feeling proud that she had run a large household as a teenager and still found the time and determination to win a scholarship, they felt she had betrayed them. After all, they had put a roof over her head, let her eat at the table with them, and furnished her with an endless supply of laundry to fill her empty hours. Then this ingrate turned her back on her own family.

When Myrna left, no one said goodbye. No one offered to take her to the railroad station. On the way out, she pinned a note to the front door that said, simply, "All of you—go to hell." From there, it was off to a world of higher learning and financial success.

As I think about Myrna and her message, I see a lot of anguish, some frustration, and obviously no small amount of hatred. It was also a most inspired message, and I think that any browbeaten and ill-used teenager who could work up the spirit to leave such a message had the stuff of success in abundant amounts.

Not that it strikes me as a message to be carved in stone and placed over the door of a high school or city library. Yet, this message cannot be totally discounted, either. As the old saying goes, if the shoe fits, wear it. We cannot escape the fact that sometimes the shoe does indeed fit, and when that happens, we can set Myrna's words to music.

The next time that a pack of distant relatives asks to drain your bank account to pay for their bad decisions, you could do a lot worse than remembering Myrna and the words of a tortured, teenage girl who became a mature woman in a matter of seconds. It is really a rather good message, succinct and honest.

The important thing to remember is that Myrna never regretted what she did, and neither does anyone else who gathers the courage for a well-aimed and sincere write-off. She said *No* to the whole family and went on to do what she had every right to do and certainly should have been doing. In your case, I suggest you try it once.

I guarantee you'll try it again.

RANDOM THOUGHTS TO GET YOU THROUGH THE DAY

When someone says he will call you right back, assume that he won't. This is the cornerstone of all human relations.

If someone doesn't deserve the truth, tell him a lie.

It is better to be bitter and vengeful than too stupid to realize it when that's the way you should feel.

Never underestimate the simpleton. Stupid people are often the most treacherous of all.

When someone has no right to make an accusation, you have every right to deny it, even when it's true.

When in doubt, go with the negative. To say that something won't work, won't happen, or won't be accepted is a much safer bet than saying that it will.

If you have nothing that anyone wants, you can afford to love mankind and trust your fellow human beings. Otherwise, don't sit with your back toward the door.

A person who likes everybody really isn't worth knowing.

People who borrow money from friends seem to be capable of only two emotions: groveling obeisance when they seek the loan, and indignation when they are asked to pay it back.

It is not always beneficial to hear the other fellow's point of view. If he is an obvious jackass, there is little to be gained from his recital of misinformation and illogical conclusions.

Those who owe us money can be very difficult to contact. The best way to communicate with them is by having a pack of angry dogs run them up a tree.

Most of our problems can be solved by the simple measure of having someone stop doing something.

No one has ever been disappointed by someone whom he didn't trust in the first place.

Those who would presume to remake the world invariably are the ones with the most difficulty replacing the eraser in the mechanical pencil.

Diplomacy is a device to give the contestants something to do until they're ready to fight, not unlike skipping rope in the dressing room.

A problem is solved only when the person with the authority to solve it wants it to be solved. Until this happens, nothing is produced but a lot of noise.

The man who craves power shouldn't have it, and the man who can handle it usually doesn't want it. This is the great dilemma of history.

Incompetence in command may not be the greatest of all human sins, but it is assuredly the most inexcusable.

A formal wedding is a prime example of man's indefatigable ability to complicate even the simplest of issues.

Please don't tell me about the brotherhood of man. I know several people whom I wouldn't accept as distant cousins.

Human progress is destined to be eternally retarded by man's insatiable passion for marching in ranks behind the banner of an imbecile.

It isn't all that difficult to make a major contribution to the betterment of mankind. Anyone who isn't now serving on a committee is helping immeasurably.

The word *activist* was coined by journalists to give them a single word to describe someone with a big mouth and no apparent job, skills, or credentials.

Industrial bureaucracy has finally brought us to the point where there is an acute shortage of nonproductive people.

No situation is ever completely hopeless. When an ordeal is played out to the end, there is always the possibility of sneaking by on a rotten hometown decision.

ABOUT THE AUTHOR

Donald G. Smith worked for over 20 years as an editor and editorial supervisor in the aerospace industry. He currently lives in Santa Maria, California, where he teaches adult writing courses and founded a writers' support group. He likes all sports (especially college football), jazz, dogs, vodka martinis, maps, corduroy, and Winslow Homer. Smith's favorite cities are San Francisco and Atlanta, and he regards Winston Churchill as the greatest human being of his lifetime.